THE ROYAL MARINES BARRACKS, EASTNEY

The
ROYAL MARINES BARRACKS,
EASTNEY

A PICTORIAL HISTORY

Andrew Lane

HALSGROVE

In association with

THE
**ROYAL
MARINES**
MUSEUM

First published in 1998 by Halsgrove
Copyright © 1998 Andrew Lane

ISBN 1 874448 93 0 (p/b)

ISBN 1 874448 92 2 (h/b)

British Library Cataloguing-in-Publication-Data
A CIP data for this book is available from the British Library

Cover illustrations reproduced by courtesy of the Royal Marines Museum, Southsea, Hants

HALSGROVE
Halsgrove House
Lower Moor Way
Tiverton EX16 6SS
T: 01884 243242
F: 01884 243325
www.halsgrove.com

Printed and bound in Great Britain
by WBC, Bridgend

Contents

Acknowledgements

The author wishes to thank all those who have assisted and supported the compilation of this book, in particular Colonel Keith Wilkins OBE, Linda Coote, Major A.J. Donald RM, Matthew Little and Sharon Bath.

All the photographs in this book are from the extensive Photographic Library of the Royal Marines Museum, except that of the West family (page 18), which was kindly lent by Mr and Mrs Harris. Grateful thanks are extended to all past donors of photographs to the Library. Without their generosity this book would not have been possible.

The Royal Marines Museum Archive and Reference Library was a valuable source of information, and thanks are also due to the staff of the Portsmouth City Record Office and the Hampshire Library Service.

To my parents

Introduction

Nostalgia is a funny thing. It can play tricks with the memory. Take, for example, the case of a young Royal Marine standing to attention in the Drill Shed at Eastney on a chilly February morning half a century ago. The drill instructor is not a happy man and his rasping voice roars around the shed. The young Marine is wishing he were anywhere but here. Fifty years later the former Marine returns to Eastney with his grandchildren. It all looks the same: the Parade Ground, the Main Block, the Clock Tower. However, he finds his way to the Drill Shed blocked by fencing. He stops a member of the museum staff, the curator, and asks if he can visit the Drill Shed. The answer brings a tear to the old man's eyes. The shed has been demolished to make way for a road to the new private residences. The veteran Marine, lost in his memories, sighs, 'Ah, the good old Drill Shed.'

At the heart of this true story is the enormous affection and nostalgia held by ex-Eastney Royal Marines. Here they made some of their best friendships; they struggled in training but they came through and became the best. They were Royal Marines, ready for sea service. From Eastney they went to join a Royal Marine Detachment on a battleship, cruiser or carrier. They toured the world or fought in theatres of operations as diverse as the Arctic and the Pacific, the North Atlantic and Korea. On their return to Portsmouth the men came back to Eastney.

For other Royal Marines, Eastney was the place where their service careers developed, whether as officers, instructors, sergeants or administrators. In some cases, their wives and families lived with them in the barracks or in the local area. There were christenings, weddings, schools, parties and concerts. Eastney Barracks was a community.

For the people of Portsmouth, especially those living at Eastney, Milton and Southsea, the presence of the Royal Marines gave a great sense of pride. They watched and cheered the ranks of immaculately turned out Royal Marines as they marched through the streets to Church Parade or to the dockyard. The local girls were equally keen. Some found husbands, others boyfriends or just a broken heart.

When the Barracks were finally closed in 1991 and the last few Royal Marines marched out behind the band, it was the end of an era and the nostalgia really began.

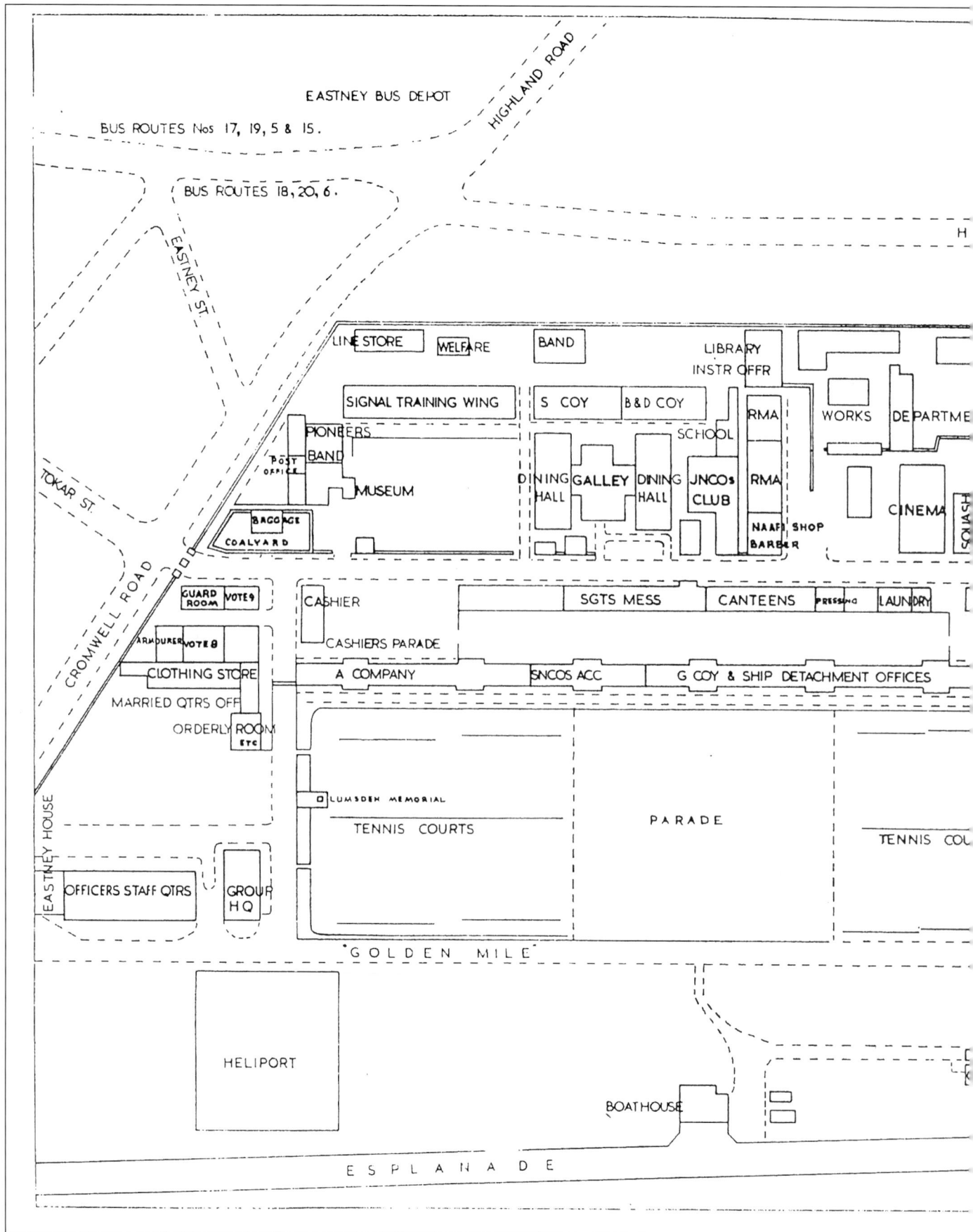

EASTNEY BUS DEPOT

HIGHLAND ROAD

BUS ROUTES Nos 17, 19, 5 & 15.

BUS ROUTES 18, 20, 6.

EASTNEY ST

TOKAR ST.

CROMWELL ROAD

EASTNEY HOUSE

LINE STORE | WELFARE | BAND | LIBRARY
INSTR OFFR

SIGNAL TRAINING WING | S COY | B & D COY | RMA | WORKS | DEPARTME

PIONEERS | BAND | SCHOOL

POST OFFICE

MUSEUM | DINING HALL | GALLEY | DINING HALL | JNCOs CLUB | RMA

RMA

NAAFI SHOP
BARBER

CINEMA

SQUASH

BAGGAGE
COALYARD

GUARD ROOM | VOTE 9 | CASHIER

CASHIERS PARADE

ARMOURER | VOTE 8

CLOTHING STORE

MARRIED QTRS OFF

ORDERLY ROOM
ETC

SGTS MESS | CANTEENS | PRESSING | LAUNDRY

A COMPANY | SNCOS ACC | G COY & SHIP DETACHMENT OFFICES

LUMSDEN MEMORIAL

TENNIS COURTS

PARADE

TENNIS COU

OFFICERS STAFF QTRS | GROUP HQ

GOLDEN MILE

HELIPORT

BOATHOUSE

ESPLANADE

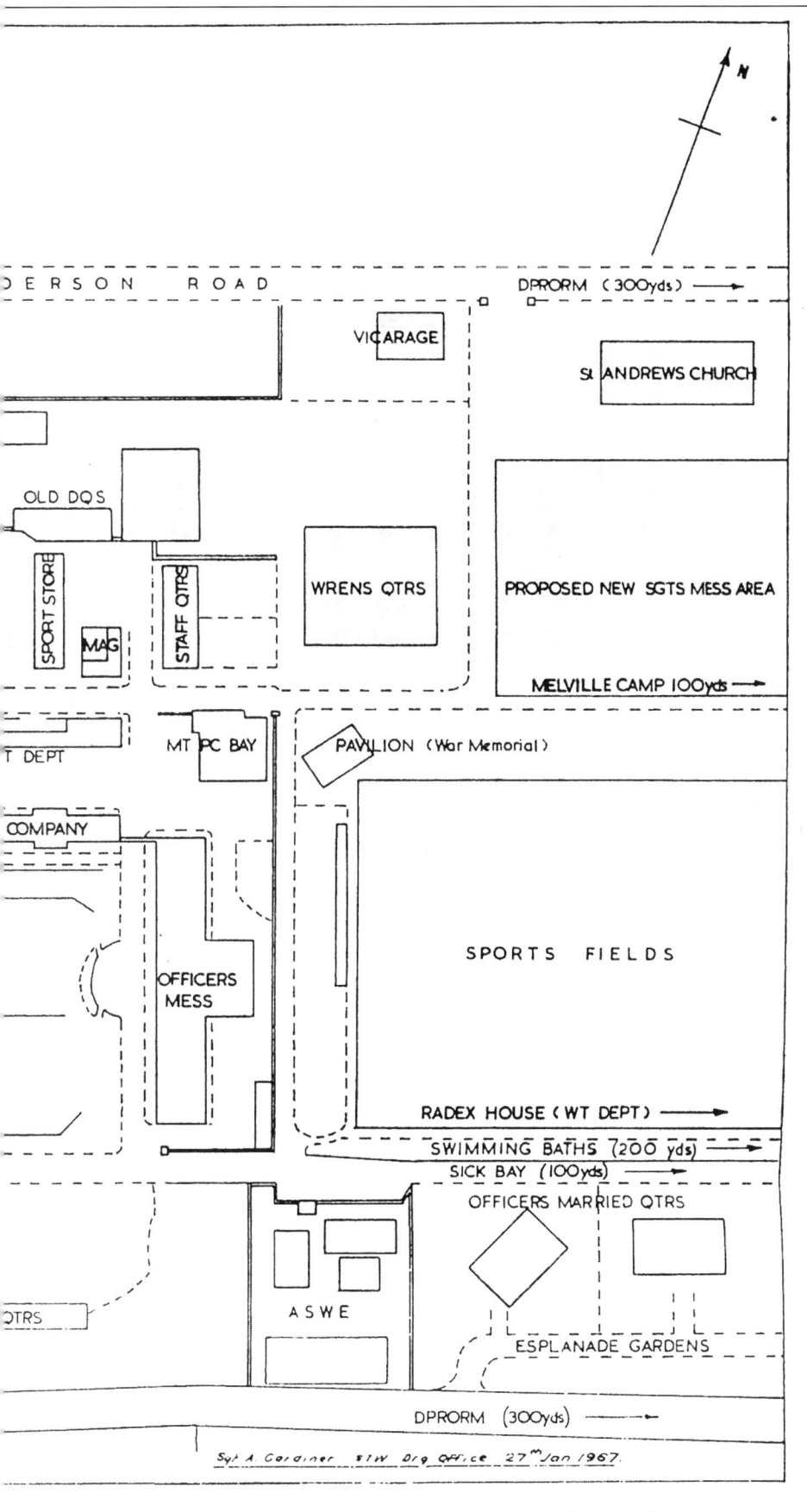

N

DERSON ROAD

DPRORM (300yds) →

VICARAGE

St ANDREWS CHURCH

OLD DQS

SPORT STORE

MAG

STAFF QTRS

WRENS QTRS

PROPOSED NEW SGTS MESS AREA

MELVILLE CAMP 100yds →

T DEPT

MT PC BAY

PAVILION (War Memorial)

COMPANY

OFFICERS MESS

SPORTS FIELDS

RADEX HOUSE (WT DEPT) →

SWIMMING BATHS (200 yds) →

SICK BAY (100yds) →

OFFICERS MARRIED QTRS

QTRS

ASWE

ESPLANADE GARDENS

DPRORM (300yds) →

Sgt A. Gardiner ∓IW Drg Office 27ᵗʰ Jan 1967.

1966 plan of the Barracks

Eastney Before the Barracks

Before the barracks were built in the 1860s, the Southsea, Milton and Eastney areas were open fields. Southsea Common was a marsh and officers travelling from Gunwharf Barracks to Fort Cumberland often took a shotgun with them in winter to shoot snipe.

Eastney village, which was no more than a few small cottages and a farm, was situated near the present caravan park. The farm was occupied in 1716 by James Osmond, a Baptist. Meetings were held at the farm and converts were baptized by immersion in the small pond near by. It was later known as Proe's Farm and Pond, after a French refugee called Proux who worked for the British during the Napoleonic War. The Duke of Kent allowed Proux to live in the farm rent free. His widow continued to live there until 1862, long after the estate had been sold to the Crown. The farmhouse was demolished in 1877 as it was too near the gun and mortar batteries. In 1925 or 1926 the pond was filled in.

What later became known as Eastney Barracks occupied the area from the present Cromwell Road to Fort Cumberland. The land was acquired in two stages. In 1845 the Crown purchased the estate, which included Eastney village, from Lady Henderson-Durham. This stretched from the present playing fields to Fort Cumberland. Between 1858 and 1860 the Henderson-Durhams sold a further 50 acres to the west, including Eastney Farm, to the War Department for the construction of a barracks complex. Eastney Barracks was to be the home of the Royal Marine Artillery.

Eastney Barracks in 1921. There is no Esplanade road, and the earthworks and ditches are still in place.

The Royal Marine Artillery

The Royal Marines were formed in 1664 and it is recorded that four years later a company of Marines were billeted in Portsmouth. In 1755 the Marines became a permanent force and were garrisoned in the Grand Divisions of Chatham, Portsmouth and Plymouth. However, there were still no barracks in Portsmouth and Marines continued to be billeted in houses, gin houses and inns – not that the men complained! With the French Revolution and Napoleonic Wars (1793–1815) the Marines increased in numbers. By 1802 there were over 30,000 and in the same year they were designated 'Royal' Marines. The great majority of Royal Marines were at sea in Nelson's battle fleets. They were used as snipers and boarding parties in sea battles and as landing parties when necessary. In 1804 an artillery company was formed at each of the Divisions to man bomb-vessels. These were barges with mortars for the bombardment of coastal defences.

It was in 1817 that

in order that they might be fully instructed in field practice and the services with projectiles, etc., Fort Monkton, situated at the Gilkicker Point, with the barracks at Haslar, were given up to them [the RMA]. Quarters were built for the officers, a mess room and an academy were formed, and the business of education immediately commenced under the able mathematical master Mr Joseph Edwards.

These quarters were not ready in time and in June 1817 four companies went to Fort Cumberland. Six months later the Royal Marine Artillery (RMA) were all together at Fort Monkton, Stokes Bay. Their stay was not without incident: an order was issued warning the men against the habit of cutting hair from the tails of the cows in the fields to make brushes for their musket locks.

In 1824 the RMA officers were in permanent accommodation in Portsmouth High Street and St Thomas's Street. The men were in the new Gunwharf site, converted for their use. Fort Cumberland was still used for training. The RMA continued to lead a nomadic existence in Portsmouth, moving between Gunwharf, Clarence Barracks and Fort Cumberland. The need for a permanent purpose-built home was agreed in 1859, when the RMA, now comprising sixteen companies, were formed into a separate division and made responsible for their own administration, pay, etc., and land at Eastney was acquired.

The Badge of the Royal Marines – colloquially known as 'the Globe and Laurel' – with their motto Per Mare Per Terram *(By sea by land). The inclusion of 'Gibraltar' on the emblem commemorates the famous capture of Gibraltar by the Royal Marines in 1704 . The 'foul anchor' is the badge of the Lord High Admiral.*

Eastney Barracks

The Building Programme

Construction of the new barracks at Eastney began in 1862. By December 1863 the contractor was complaining of the inconvenience caused by numerous Marines, in some cases accompanied by their wives and families, wishing to view the men's quarters (the main block facing onto the parade ground).

The first controversy now arose over the Eastney project. There was some confusion over the design of the site: was it a fort or barracks? A description of the time states:

> The Barracks will stand on an extensive piece of ground, and its front will have a long defensive work consisting of a long curtain (bank) with a heavy work at either end (Eastney Fort East and Fort West) in line with the sea beach, each containing two guns in cavalier bastions, and seven guns in embrasures. The whole is fronted and flanked by a deep ditch, having a low wall next to the scarp of the work for rifle fire. The scarp of the work itself is reverted with flints and concrete.

However, questions were asked in the House of Commons about the wisdom of the design. In May 1864 Colonel Bartlett stood up in the Commons to say he thought the barracks were in a most 'untenable position' in the event of an attack from the sea. He thought it would have been safer for the men and their wives and families if the barracks had been built further inland, as the small forts might be bomb-proof but not three-storey barrack blocks. The Colonel ended by stating that private houses had been allowed to be built close to the barracks. They were vulnerable too.

Lord Paget, for the Government, replied that it was a good site for heavy guns and the men should reside near by. Besides, the site had been obtained by the Admiralty, 'at very little expense'. The Spitbank Forts in the Solent, when finished, would offer protection.

Sir F. Smith said he thought he had never seen barracks worse situated – and they would cost £167,861 to build. Lord Paget confirmed that the estimate for building the barracks was £167,000, and added that if there was a war the men of the RMA would be at sea. The Opposition mocked this weak argument, protesting that the men might be gone but their wives and children would be left undefended.

Despite their flawed design, the construction of the barracks went ahead.

On 7 November 1864 the first detachment (from Fort Elson) marched in, but it was not until 1 April 1865 that the portion that had been completed was handed over to the Barrack Master. It appears the Main Block, the Guardroom block and the Married Quarters were available. The Married Quarters (later the Signal School, and now Lidiard Gardens) accommodated 92 families. Other ranks were permitted only one room and as some men had six children (one had nine), there was not enough room. Older children slept in dormitories.

The Officers' Mess was completed at the end of 1865. The field officers' quarters (Teapot Row) were built in 1866, as was the Commandant's office. This block was known as 'Scandal Alley'.

By 1867 the RMA had fully moved into the barracks. The Married Quarters and School were north of the main block. The Drill Shed, Detention Quarters and Officers' Stables had also been built.

The sewers were defective at first and typhoid caused several deaths. In consequence, a ventilation shaft and chimney were built between the parade ground and the sea. In 1868 Surgeon Robertson RN had condemned the Eastney Barracks area in a report, 'Health of the Navy'. He criticized:

> the unwholesomeness and pestilential character of the dwellings in the neighbourhood of the barracks, which are almost wholly occupied by families belonging to Marine Artillerymen.... In one street not a single house has a drain except into a piece of waste ground at the end of the row of houses. Some had a cesspool within a few yards of the back door.

The whole of the Eastney Barracks site, stretching from the Clock Tower (left) to Fort Cumberland at the mouth of Langstone Harbour, 1973

The basic accommodation was all there by 1867 and further facilities were added. In 1869 the parade ground was completed. The Water Tower followed in 1870–71. Originally built to provide the necessary force of water for the fire mains, it was later converted to a clock tower. The clock was made in 1784 by William Dutton, London, and was formerly the Woolwich Dockyard clock.

Then came the Carpenters' Shop and Shooting Gallery (1886) and the Blacksmiths' Shop (1887). In 1890 the wooden floor of the Drill Shed was replaced with asphalt. Soon afterwards a roller-skating club was formed there. The Band Practice Room and Tailor's Shop were set up in 1892, and the bowling alley was converted into a billiard room for the men in 1895. In 1898 the Gymnasium was built.

The Commandant's horse and carriage outside his quarters (Eastney House) in 1890

The West family outside No. 4 Teapot Row, Eastney, in 1920

An unidentified group of Eastney Royal Marines and domestic staff, 1884

The Commandant's Quarters, c. 1902

The back entrance to Teapot Row (the field officers' quarters), c. 1890.

Croquet and tennis behind Teapot Row, c. 1900

RMA officers on the steps of Teapot Row, c. 1890

Ceremonial parade by the RMA at Eastney for the birthday of HM Queen Victoria, 24 May 1869. The original Married Quarters (left) later became the RN School of Music before becoming the Signals School.

One of the first photographs taken of the new Eastney Barracks, this shows the Royal Marine Artillery on parade in 1869.

A ceremonial parade in 1902 with a rare view of the earthworks, main drainage ventilation chimney and boathouse

The Water Tower, later the Clock Tower, a few years after the opening of Eastney Barracks

The Gymnasium, c. 1910

Bayonet fencing training for RMA recruits in the Gymnasium, 1908

The Drill Shed, c. 1910.

The men's Library, c. 1904

The main gate, c. 1904. The central pillar was removed in 1966 to allow coaches to enter and a clear way for learner truck drivers.

Outside the Guardroom, c. 1904

View of the Guardroom and the main East-West road through the Barracks, c. 1900

Theatre

The New Theatre, later known as the Globe, was built in 1899, replacing the original wooden building that had been used for thirty years. In the first performance in the New Theatre there were seventeen variety acts, which included an orchestral band, solo singers, a performer with Indian clubs, mandolinists, a comedian, a violin soloist and a dramatic farce. The theatre was open only during the winter, offering entertainment in the form of plays, smoking concerts and band concerts. By 1921, however, the theatre was also being used as a cinema; this continued for many decades.

An inspector's report on the redevelopment of Eastney in 1947 described it as 'a galvanised covered building of inadequate seating capacity. Badly planned with poor sight lines, acoustics bad.'

The theatre footlights were probably gaslight, but it was not long before electric lighting was installed. Electricity came to Eastney Barracks in 1904, when 3000 lamps were fitted. In the same year a telephone exchange was installed in the Guardroom.

V. R.

ROYAL MARINE ARTILLERY THEATRE.

Under the Patronage of COLONEL H. ADAIR, Commandant, and the OFFICERS of the
Royal Marine Artillery.

A Special Performance for Officers & their Friends

WILL TAKE PLACE

ON FRIDAY, NOVEMBER 29TH, 1878.

On this occasion will be produced an entirely New and Original Comedy by F. C. BURNAUD, ESQ.,
entitled—

OUR CLUB?

STANISLAUS RADETSKI, (an Englishman of Hungarian extraction, Architect and Artist,
Member of the Eccentric Club) ... ... Capt. E. J. NOBLE.
ALFONSE DUBUISON, (a naturalized Frenchman, Poet and Painter, Secretary of the
Eccentric Club) ... ... Lieut. W. C. NICHOLLS.
HENRY LENNARD, (*alias* Gurdon, Artist & Actor, Member of the Eccentric Club) Capt. H. EVERITT
Dr. STANMORE, (retired Physician, Member of the Eccentric Club) ... Lieut. G. D. RAITT.
CAPTAIN RANGER, R.N. } Members of the {Capt. W. La T. COCKRAFT.
CAPTAIN FARNBOROUGH,} Eccentric Club. {Lieut. L. T. PEASE.
BUFFLEY, (Steward of the Eccentric Club) ... ... Capt. G. F. PENGELLEY.
ROBERT, (Servant of the Eccentric Club) ... ... Capt. W. MILLER.
TOM RIPPENDALE, (Gardener at the Priory) ... ... Capt. G. F. PENGELLEY.
HON. RICHARD FROBISHER ... ... Capt. GRAHAM, 105th Regt.
LADY CRAWFORD ... ... Mrs. H. B. TUSON.
MRS. DUBUISON ... ... Miss GRAHAM.
MRS. WRAY, (of the Priory, Maplehurst) ... ... Mrs. R. C. ALLEN.
MISS NELLIE GURDON, (Henry Lennard's Sister) ... ... MISS KATE WHITE.

The action of the piece takes place between 10.30 a.m. and 6 p.m. the same day.

Act. I.—MORNING ROOM IN THE ECCENTRIC CLUB. Getting into a Tangle.

Act. II.—DRAWING ROOM AT THE PRIORY, MAPLEHURST. Entanglement.

Act. III.—THE PRIORY RUINS. Unravelling.

Manager, CAPT. W. LA T. COCKRAFT. Stage Manager, MAJOR H. B. TUSON. Prompter, CAPT. G. F. PENGELLEY.

ADMISSION BY TICKET ONLY.

Doors open at 7.30 P.M. Commence at 8 P.M. Carriages at 10.15 P.M.

*The STRING BAND of the Corps under the direction of Mr. J. WINTERBOTTOM, will
perform the following Music during the Evening :—*

OVERTURE ... ... " Giralda " ... ... Adam.
SELECTION ... From the New Opera " Carmen" ... ... Biret.
FANTASIA ... ... " Fatinitza " ... ... Suppé.

VIVAT REGINA!

Charpentier, Portsmouth.

Programme for a performance given at the first RMA theatre at Eastney in 1878

An RMA concert party in the Edwardian era

The replacement Globe Theatre lasted from 1899 to the 1970s.

Drill and Recreation

Physical training and recreation were catered for by the Drill Field, the Swimming Baths and various sports facilities. The present sports field was originally the Drill Field. It was actually an arable field and belonged to Farmer Joliffe, whose farm extended to the north beyond the present Henderson Road. Officers in the Mess could look out of the east-facing windows, over the flint wall, to see the men performing drill. When the Kaiser visited the Officers' Mess he watched a mock attack carried out over these fields. In 1889 the Portsmouth Corporation wanted ground east of Fort Cumberland for an outfall and tanks for their drainage system. The Corporation bought the farm fields behind the Officers' Mess from Joliffe and exchanged them with the Admiralty for the ground beyond the Fort.

Land totalling 33 acres was now adapted for sports facilities and as the site for a new church. In 1890 the Cricket Ground was created with 40 tons of chalk obtained from Paulsgrove chalk pit. The remaining area was laid to grass as a drill field. The original defensive work beyond the flint wall behind the Officers' Mess, comprising a redoubt and ditch, was levelled and filled in in 1898. A football ground was built on this site and it was ready for the 1902–3 season. Further additions were the Sergeants' Tennis Courts and a sports pavilion.

The Swimming Baths were built in a hollow where there had been a natural lake. Built in 1904 by Samuel Slater of Yorke Street, Southsea, the pool measured 65 feet by 28 feet and had concrete 4 feet thick in the base and walls. It was filled with sea water. Lack of insulation was a problem; the concrete flat roof caused such a rain of condensation that spectators had to wear raincoats.

Water polo team in the Swimming Baths, c. 1911

Sick Quarters

The original Infirmary for the barracks was constructed in Eastney Fort East in 1866. This proved inadequate and a new purpose-built one replaced it in 1881; it remained until the 1970s. A disinfector was installed and, following the 1918 influenza epidemic, the Spraying Chamber was built. The Infirmary was a rather grim place and a 1947 inspector's report condemned it as inadequate and below modern standards.

A Dispensary and Women's Waiting Room were created in the northern section of the barracks, by the School. Highland House was the 'sick house' for married families between 1892 and 1904, after which date a house in Highland Road was used.

The Infirmary in 1973

The School

Eastney Barracks School, opened in 1867, was situated in the northern part of the Barracks, near the main gate. It was used by the children of the Marines and by the men themselves. To raise standards all Royal Marine recruits were ordered to attend school on specified days until they had obtained their First- or Second-Class Certificate.

For the children, the School was divided into three departments – boys, girls and infants – making an average population of 500 pupils. The staff of the Girls' and Infants' Schools were female civilians but the boys had Royal Marine instructors. It was also the practice to have pupil teachers, who were unqualified and paid £5 to £13 a year (1885 wages).

After 1894, when the School was placed under inspection by the Education Department, it reflected typical Victorian school life. Attendance was enforced until ten years of age, the leaving age being raised to twelve in 1899. The School received a Government grant under a system known as 'payments by results'. The grant was calculated on attendance figures, test results and an annual inspection. For example, the Eastney Barracks Girls' School logbook for July 1902 reported the annual grant per child was 22s., making a total annual grant of £143 based on their annual attendance figures. It is hardly surprising therefore that the School placed such emphasis on pupils attending regularly.

Outbreaks of childhood illnesses could decimate the annual attendance figures. The Eastney School logbooks record epidemics of measles, mumps and influenza. Disease and lice infestation would cause the Schools to be closed down for fumigation, as happened in January 1921; the logbook records: 'Orders received from Medical Officer that children and teachers are to attend at the Spraying Chamber for disinfection each morning at 11.15 am until further orders.' The spraying was discontinued on 1 March.

The subjects taught at the School at the turn of the century were religious knowledge, grammar, English history, writing, reading, arithmetic, geography, singing, poetry and drill (PE). The girls also learnt needlework and their work was sold to raise funds for the School each year. From 1891 the older girls from Eastney Barracks School attended the Bramble Road School for cookery classes. The inspectors consistently found the School to be run to a high standard of discipline and organization. In 1891 one inspector noted: 'Reading has improved, but the phrasing requires attention and it should be realised that reading is not merely a mechanical art but a means of gaining knowledge.' In 1910 the inspector of the Boys' School was not happy that there were four classes and four teachers, all being taught in one undivided room.

The Barracks School's year was punctuated by the usual holidays but it also reflected the era and its location. There were days off for royal coronations, weddings and funerals. There was a holiday in June 1902 for 'Peace in South Africa' after the Boer War, and others for VIP visits and sports events.

By 1921 the day of the elementary schools was coming to an end. In March the children of Royal Marines who were not actually serving (i.e. pensioners) were excluded; this did not include children whose fathers had died while serving. Some staff were laid off. On 21 December 1921 the three elementary schools closed down and the children were transferred to the local school in Milton. Thereafter, only serving ranks were taught there. In 1958 the Royal Marines Museum was established in the School building before moving to larger premises in the Officers' Mess in 1975. The School building was finally demolished in 1983.

The Churches

The first church at Eastney Barracks was known as the Crinoline Church, because of its distinctive circular roof. This wooden building was originally constructed as a mobile field hospital for the Crimean War.

The 'Crinoline Church', Eastney Barracks, around the turn of the century

However, it became instead a temporary church for the parish of St Simon and St Bartholomew in Portsmouth before moving to Eastney in 1864. It was sited to the west of Teapot Row (near the present Marine Court). The twenty-sided Crinoline Church could accommodate a congregation of 950 but with a Barracks population of 1800, a new and larger permanent church was planned in 1901.

The Crinoline Church (left), west of Teapot Row

In 1902 a sum of £10,000 was allowed for the building of St Andrew's Church, adjacent to Henderson Road. On 16 March 1904, HRH The Prince of Wales, as Colonel in Chief of the Royal Marines, and the Princess of Wales came to Eastney to lay the church's foundation stone. This was a large and well-orchestrated event. Following visits to some areas of the Barracks, a Parade Ground Review and lunch in the Officers' Mess, the stone-laying ceremony began. There were forty clergy, a band, a choir, a guard of honour and over two thousand spectators, including the RMA schoolchildren. It was the Princess of

St Andrew's Church, Eastney, in 1917

The interior of St Andrew's Church, with the reredos behind the altar

Wales who actually laid the foundation stone. Under the stone was placed a casket of papers and coins.

Construction of the church continued for a further eighteen months; it was dedicated in November 1905 by the Bishop of Winchester. Measuring 218 feet long, 48 feet high and 66 feet wide, it could accommodate a congregation of 1000, a smaller capacity than anticipated. The building was made of Rowlands Castle red brick with Portland and Bath stone dressings. The chancel and altar steps were of Sicilian marble. The altar roof was oak and the rest of the roof of pine. Radiators and electric lights were fitted.

Over the remaining 68 years of its life as a church there were further embellishments to the building, mainly memorials. In 1920 a reredos (a screen at the back of the altar) was erected to the memory of the RMA killed in the Great War. It was dedicated and unveiled by Major General Sir A. Paris KCB. A memorial to Paris himself was unveiled in 1939.

The 1914–18 memorial was moved in 1963 to a newly created Chapel of Remembrance, which included a 1939–45 memorial. This move was necessary because the reredos obscured the stained-glass windows behind the altar. These windows were the RMA memorial to the fallen of South Africa and China (1899–1902). The Book of Remembrance and all memorial plaques were moved into the Chapel and the South Wall of the church.

The church was as busy in its activities as any parish church. There were Sunday Schools, a Choir, a Church of England Men's Society, Mothers' Union, Lads' Bible Class and Youth Club and also a Guild of Servers. The Sunday Church Parade was a major event, still fondly remembered by the residents of Eastney and Milton.

In 1973 St Andrew's closed and the premises were used as the Band's practice room. In 1997–8 the former church was converted into private residences.

St Andrew's after the modifications of 1963

St Andrew's Church Choir, 1920

The choir in 1969

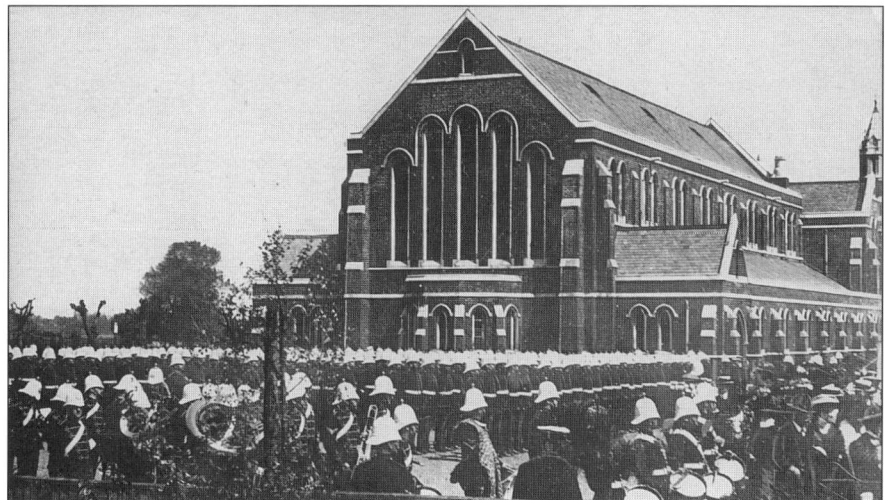

Church Parade at St Andrew's

The Sergeants' Mess

In the Victorian era the Marine Sergeants were billeted with their men in barrack rooms. Married NCOs had the privilege of having their wives live with them in the room. They were normally allocated 'the corner bedspace' and allowed to rig up a canvas screen for privacy. In July 1904 a new Sergeants' Mess was opened on the main East-West Road; in 1967 this became the JNCOs' (Junior NCOs') Club. In 1911 the SNCOs (Senior NCOs) were given separate living quarters in cubicles in C Block of the Main Block.

In 1967 the new Sergeants' Mess was opened, between the Playing Fields and St Andrew's Church. After the 1973 constriction of the Barracks, the accommodation was taken over by the Headquarters Training Group for use by all ranks.

The Sergeants' Billiard Room, c. 1908

The RMA Sergeants' Mess, 1904

The Sergeants' Mess laid out for a formal dinner, 1921

The sergeants' annual outing, c. 1920

The Officers' Mess

At the eastern end of the Parade Ground and lawns stood the magnificent Officers' Mess, now the home of the Royal Marines Museum. The building was completed in 1865 with the Mess in the centre and adjoining wings of 'cabins' (single rooms). The Mess functioned until 1973 and some cabins until 1991.

The external stone staircase bears the scars of previous Guest Night escapades when small field guns, kept in the hall, were taken out to the lawns. Entering the Mess, the Ante-Room was on the left and the Breakfast Room on the right. Each contained marble fireplaces made by Italian craftsmen, and mirrors and fine paintings. Jumping onto the mantelpiece in the Ante-Room on Guest Nights was a particular party piece of General Alan Bourne's. The fireplace (which still survives) is 4 feet 3 inches (131 cm) high.

Before 1923, when the amalgamation of the RMA and the RMLI (Royal Marine Light Infantry) caused an increase in the number of officers at Eastney, only dinner was served in the Mess room. All other meals were served in the Breakfast Room. Second Lieutenants took tea in the Breakfast Room, while other officers had their tea in the Ante-Room. Later a cocktail bar was installed in the Breakfast Room.

In the Hall, with its imposing staircase, were the trophies and the medal collection. The ironwork on the staircase incorporates the clear anchor, the badge of the Lord High Admiral. There are no Royal Navy fouled-anchor emblems in any of the Mess architecture.

The three windows at the top of the stairs were, until 1944, of stained glass, representing Faith, Hope and Charity. They were removed to make the Hall lighter. Traditionally no Royal Marine officer ever descended the right-hand staircase, since this meant facing the Charity window, and no Royal Marine officer looks charity in the face.

The painting of George III by Northcote on the staircase is one of only two equestrian portraits of him known to exist, the other being in the Crown Court, Lancaster. Despite their grandeur, the stairs were not exempt from the hazards of officers' horseplay. Tobogganing down the stairs on trays was an popular pastime. Major Aston, recently returned from the Boer War, careered down without taking off his spurs; the carpet was cut to threads.

Upstairs in the Mess were the Card Room (now replaced by a lift shaft and part of the Royal Marines Band Exhibition), the Library (which now houses the Royal Marines Band Exhibition), the Billiard Room (now the Medal Room) and the Minstrels' Gallery, where musicians played for Guest Night dinners. From the 1920s, when cards were permitted to be played in the Ante-Room, the Card Room was also used for entertaining private guests The Library once held a considerable collection but it was thinned out in the early 1950s. There were two tables in the Billiard Room; the cue cupboard is still in place.

The main dining room, the Mess Room, is the centre-piece of the whole building. The ceiling and mouldings are particularly fine and the fireplaces are of Italian marble. The Italian craftsmen left their mark by sculpting the Corps' motto incorrectly; it reads 'Per Mare Per Tere' (instead of 'Terram'). There are two fine crests between the balcony windows, one of the royal arms and the other of the Royal Marine Artillery.

The Conservatory was built in 1894 on to the alcove of the Mess Room. It looked out onto the original Drill Field, now the football pitches. It gave an excellent view and was used as an observation point by the Kaiser to watch a demonstration of a smoke attack by Royal Marines advancing from Fort Cumberland. The painting of Queen Victoria was copied from the original by H. von Angeli by Herman G. Herkomer Junior and purchased by the RMA in 1886.

Life in the Officers' Mess was ruled by traditions and rituals. A newly arrived young officer had to learn the conventions quickly in order to be accepted. In the Victorian and Edwardian eras there was a harsh hierarchy in the Mess. Promotion was slow and there was a tendency to marry late in life. Many very senior Majors and Lieutenant Colonels lived in and they could be intolerant of young officers who did not know their place. As late as the Second World War only foolhardy young officers dared to approach the carpet in front of the hearth, which was strictly reserved for field officers. Even taking the only copy of *The Times* was not advisable if there was the slightest chance that some senior officer had not seen it.

The wrath of martinets was not the only worry for lowly Second Lieutenants. The cost of mess living was high and beyond the means of their pay of 5/3 a day. In 1918 the daily mess charges were 2/6 for breakfast, 2/6 for lunch, 1/6 for tea and 3/6 for dinner. Full meals cost 10/- a day. Young officers who were unable to afford all these costly meals bought food from the Canteen or elsewhere and their

The Officers' Mess, c. 1902

Officers of the Royal Marine Artillery, 1907

attendants cooked it for them. Breakfast was taken in the officers' own quarters. Before 1914, a further cost they had to meet was the provision of livery for their personal batman. For the RMA officer's attendant, this consisted of a dark blue tail coat, scarlet waistcoat, blue plush breeches, white stockings, black leather shoes with large silver buckles, a white shirt, collar and tie and white gloves. This livery was worn only at dinner. At other meals a jean jacket and waistcoat were worn with a butterfly collar, starched shirt front and black bow-tie.

The officer also had to provide his own mess dress. For the RMA until 1914 this was particularly splendid. The blue overalls had gold stripes of Marine Corps pattern lace down the seams and were surmounted by a blue jacket and scarlet waistcoat. The coat had a stiff upright collar of scarlet bordered with gold lace carrying the grenade badges on each side. Intricately woven gold lace, which varied according to rank, adorned the cuffs. The jacket and waistcoat were edged with gold lace and a row of brass buttons. Wellington boots were worn, and before 1902 mounted officers wore spurs. After the Great War the elaborate mess dress was replaced by a plain blue jacket with a blue waistcoat and overalls with broad red stripes. One Eastney tradition arose from this ornate RMA mess dress. It was a custom when applauding after dinner to strike the table from underneath because the heavy gold lace in the sleeves would have scratched the polished surface of the table.

Until the mid-1920s the only living-quarter furnishings supplied by the Admiralty were fire irons, coal scuttles, Chesterfield tables, Windsor chairs and bedstead mattresses. Floorboards were bare. Officers often hired furnishings from civilian firms such as Jeeps of High Street, Portsmouth.

There were coal fires in the cabins, but Eastney Officers' Mess is remembered by many as a chilly, unwelcoming place. General Blumberg recalls: 'The Eastney Mess room used to be the coldest and most uncomfortable room in the kingdom; in the winter the senior officers used to dine in their greatcoats, whilst the rest of us sat and shivered.' In 1947 an official report on the modernization of Eastney Barracks reported: 'The Officers' Mess is an example of the Victorian grand manner in planning and design. It is over-large, comfortless, it has a cheerless, repellent atmosphere and arouses but little local enthusiasm.' It was not a Mess for the modern Corps.

If Eastney Officers' Mess was the product of an imperial age, then the Edwardian garden party was its showpiece. The Officers' Garden Party of July 1900 is just one example among many. The party was held on the front lawn of the Mess. Five hundred people were present and food was served in the Mess and in several marquees. There were sideshows for younger guests. The bicycle was all the rage at the time and there were several events using this form of transport, such as the officers' lemon-cutting competition, the ladies' bending race, where they rode around bottles, and the whistling race for ladies and gentleman in pairs (here, each lady cycled to the line of men and handed an envelope to her partner; he opened the envelope and whistled the tune named on the card inside). In addition, there was croquet and golf putting, a shooting gallery, coconut shies and an Aunt Sally stall. In glorious sunshine, with ladies and parasols, the Officers' Garden Party was a quintessentially English event.

The Mess Room (the main dining-room in the Officers' Mess), c. 1932

The east side of the Mess Room

Fire drill outside the Officers' Quarters and Mess, 1907

A garden party held by the RMA officers for the Imperial Japanese Navy, 1907

The officers' tennis courts, 1902

RMA officers outside their Mess, 1904

Daily Life in the Barracks

By 1871 there were 1162 servicemen at Eastney, 306 of whom lived outside the Barracks. It was a thriving community with a whole range of trades and duties to support the Barracks' work. The 1878 Standing Orders for the RMA record that there was a carpenter, a blacksmith, a lamplighter, a coal meter, a storeman, gardeners, armourers, Pioneers (general-duty Marines), tailors, shoemakers, boats crew, cooks, nurses, schoolmasters and schoolmistresses at the Barracks.

The general working hours were 6 am to 6 pm with an hour for breakfast and one and a half hours for dinner in summer, and 8 am to 6 pm with one hour for dinner in winter.

In the Shoemaker's Shop boots were made by hand and repairs undertaken. The shop lasted from 1885 to 1939, after which the work was contracted out to merchants.

Hundreds of women used to take away cloth and other materials from the Tailor's Shop every day and return with the finished articles. Each article was cut out ready for them to sew together. The master tailor paid a fixed price per dozen articles. The Shoemaker's Shop operated in the same manner until 1939.

For a Gunner daily life was very ordered. A typical day in 1907 began with reveille at 05.00 and parade at 06.00 for a short march up to Fort Cumberland. After breakfast, all ranks were detailed off for instruction, either in infantry drill on the parade ground, Repository drill (moving dismantled artillery) at Fort Cumberland, or musketry on the range. This lasted until 13.00. Infantry drill was interspersed with vigorous PT with rifles. In the afternoon, the entire Barracks turned to for fatigues until 16.30. On Saturday mornings, as a variation, the whole battalion paraded and marched out to an area such as Bedhampton.

There was no dining hall then and meals were taken in the barrack rooms under canteen messing. Breakfast consisted of black coffee and bread, while lunch was three-quarters of a pound of meat. (For those out on the rifle range, lunch was bullock's head soup, sold from a handcart for a penny a mug.) If there was any bread left over, this was served at tea at 16.30. There was no supper and no further food was issued until morning drill, at which it was not uncommon for men to faint. These were the basic rations, and ranks paid a certain amount each week for the extras.

Money was always in short supply. In 1887 a Gunner's pay was a shilling and twopence a day with a penny beer money. Sevenpence a day was deducted for rations (meat, bread, tea, coffee, milk, sugar, potatoes and vegetables). In 1904 free bread and meat was introduced and twopence halfpenny's worth of groceries.

The clothing issue was meagre and the men were constantly having to find the money to replace their kit. In 1887 NCOs and men were issued with a blue tunic once every two years, a blue kersey (everyday uniform), a pair of tweed trousers, a flannel shirt, a pair of boots and a pillbox cap. The RMLI wore scarlet tunics and kerseys instead of blue and a glengarry instead of a pillbox cap. The kersey was worn for all drills, parades and walking out, except Review Order (ceremonial inspections, where best uniform was required).

The daily routine for certain types of officer was in complete contrast to that of the Gunners. In 1889 Sir George Aston described the system there as 'admirable':

in fact so good in its way, that to spend more than a year there as a field officer without any responsibility was about as soul-killing an experience as it is possible to devise. Apart from revising my knowledge of drill I don't think my duties could have occupied on average more than about two hours a day. They consisted chiefly of inspecting and sampling bread, and sitting on Boards to survey clothing, equipment and every conceivable sort of store or supply, from a broom-handle to a truss of hay.

A view from the Clock Tower over the Main Accommodation Block to the Officers' Mess, c. 1868

Gunners Walk, on the south side of the main block, around the turn of the century

A barrack room, with the beds neatly stowed away

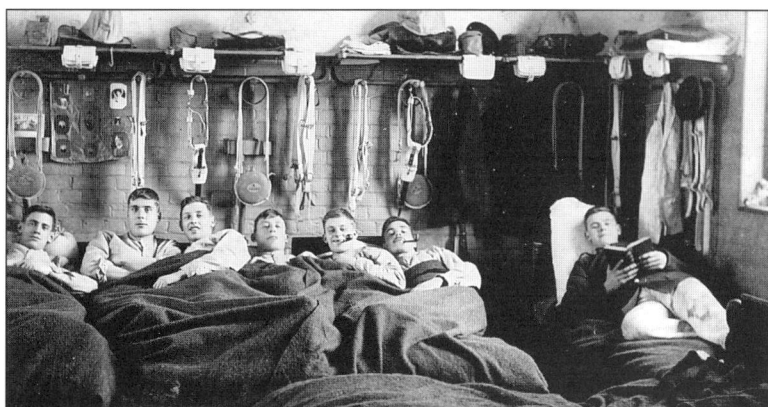

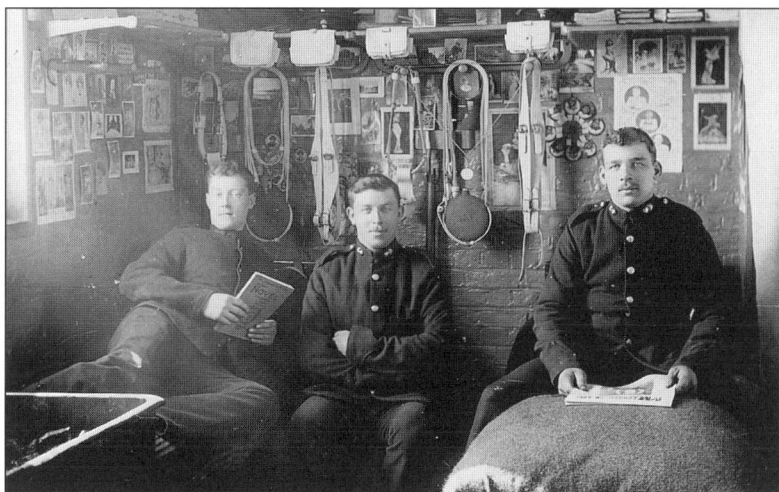

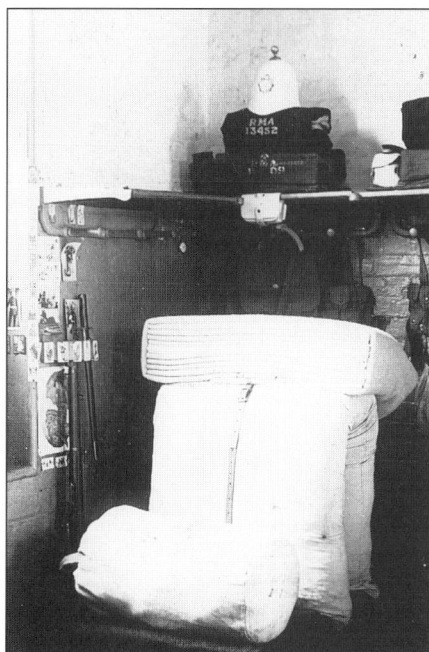

More scenes inside the men's barracks, c. 1908

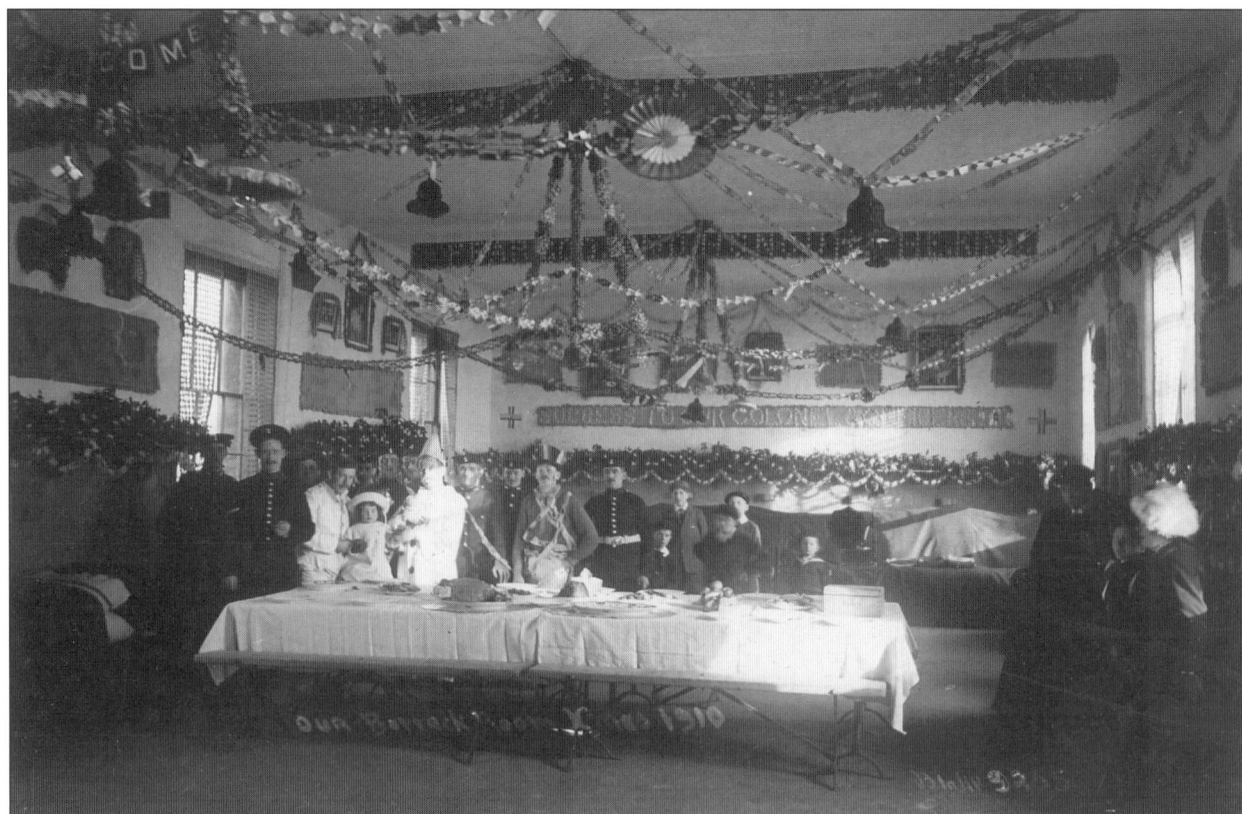

Christmas Day 1910 in the barracks

A rather more austere Christmas Day, 1918

Men of the RMA in 1916 ...

... and in 1920

The Other Ranks' Billiard Room, c. 1911

The cookhouse for the main block

During the First World War, the RMA held a fair on their drill field to raise money for war charities.

A wartime version of the fairground shy. Participants at the Eastney Fair of 1917 are invited to knock off the hat of a dummy conscientious objector.

Royal Marines and their families at the hoop-la stall at the fair

Nell's grave in Gunners Walk, Eastney (now in the grounds of the museum). Nell was a dog who befriended the RMA when they first landed at Alexandria in 1882 and followed them into several battles during the Egyptian campaign. When the Royal Marines embarked for England she swam out to their ship and returned with them to Eastney. Such was the affection for Nell that a silver collar and miniature medals were made for her to wear when she attended parades.

RMA Separation Allowance staff, 1915. (The man on the right looks particularly bored with the paperwork.)

Men of the RMA on a driver-training course, c. 1910, in the days before electric starters and front-wheel brakes

The Parade Ground with the RMA formed up for review, c. 1904

The Canteen, c. 1904: for the men, the focus of most of their social life

A scene of comradeship in the courtyard of the Canteen, where the Gunners could spend their daily 1d. beer allowance

The Artists' Rifle Corps, visiting Eastney in 1908, march off the Parade Ground to church behind the RMA Band.

Amalgamation and War

In the years immediately after the First World War, the Royal Marines faced a crisis. The government called for a reduction of the Corps to just 6000 men from the wartime high of 55,000. A compromise was reached and, to retain 9500 men, in 1923 the Corps agreed to amalgamate the RMA with the RMLI at Gosport. The RMLI would move over to Eastney and Forton Barracks, Gosport, would close. This amalgamation inevitably meant a period of transition; they might both be part of the same Corps but the rivalry between the RMA and the RMLI was intense.

By the time of the Second World War, Eastney was still a premier base. The main role of the Royal Marine Corps, Sea Service, continued to be the Barracks' principal training function. The atmosphere of the Barracks was one of confidence and activity. When war was declared on 3 September 1939 the Orderly Officer reported the news to the senior officer in the Mess and requested his orders. The reply was succinct: 'Shut the White Gate.' (This gate, mainly used by the officers, was at the end of a long road through the Barracks, by Teapot Row.) So the war began for Eastney.

To cope with the influx of new recruits, a camp of huts was built behind St Andrew's Church, henceforth known as Hutment Camp.

Although the Barracks survived the 1939–45 war virtually unscathed (but see the account of a bombing raid on page 116), there was one incident of note. One afternoon in August 1942 two squads were rehearsing ceremonial drill on the Parade Ground. Suddenly two German fighter planes appeared above the Officers' Mess and began to strafe the parade ground, wounding a number of men. An NCO named Alfred Hewitt ordered his squad (167 HO) to 'Open order march' to create space between the ranks. As

The 12th Battalion Royal Marines on parade before embarking for Shanghai in 1927

the wounded were being carried to the Drill Shed by their colleagues of 176 (Regulars) Squad, the second plane opened fire and bullets flew all around Hewitt. Miraculously, he was not hit; he managed to look up, and saw the German gunner in the forward turret. Once inside the Drill Shed the men heard a loud explosion outside the Barracks. The clock face shattered and the clock stopped, reading 2.50. Alfred Hewitt was later recommended for commissioning as an officer and became a lieutenant.

The experience of being a new recruit at Eastney during the war is clearly remembered by former Royal Marine Archibald Clarke. He recalls how the Drill Shed was used as the Reception Centre for recruits; tables were set up to dispense room and squad numbers. The Recruit Block was 'a prison-like building' of three storeys. The ground floor housed the toilets and bath-washrooms. From the entrance a wide stone staircase with black-painted hand-rails climbed in flights of ten to the top. All the rooms were of the same pattern and size, with high white ceilings, green walls and brown lino floors. In the centre of each room a pot-bellied stove stood on a steel plate. The solid iron beds with palliasses of woven steel bases 'could have been the original ones', Clarke comments. There was a long rifle rack in the centre of the room, and a wooden shelf over each bed completed the furniture. The recruit of 1939 and the recruit of 1902 had a lot in common.

The air raid shelters built around the Parade Ground in 1940 can still be seen in this 1953 scene.

The only known photograph of a team from the Royal Marine Boom Patrol Detachment (RMBPD), who were later immortalized in the film Cockleshell Heroes. *They are seen here training off Southsea beach before their raid on shipping at Bordeaux in December 1942. Of the ten men who canoed ashore, only two survived the raid.*

Men of 'A' Troop, 1st Anti-Tank Battery, at Eastney in April 1943

An advertisement from 1946

WRNS

The outbreak of the Second World War saw the return to the Barracks of the WRNS, who had served at Eastney in 1917 and 1918. They would remain for the next fifty years. WRNS attached to Royal Marine units were often referred to as 'Marens'.

The first intake of WRNS at Eastney, 1917

Pay Office Staff at Eastney, 1918

Inspection by the Commandant of WRNS in 1948 on Eastney Parade Ground

March Past by the WRNS, 1948

WRNS, Eastney Barracks, c. 1948, including Ruth Dunn (seventh from right, second row from top) and Rosemary Nicholson (standing, bottom row, second from right)

WRNS, Eastney, July 1960

Some of the last WRNS at Eastney, October 1982. Left to right, back row: Wren A. Hankinson, Wren K. Brown, L/Wren K. Freeman, L/Wren K. Grainger; middle row: Wren A. Casey, L/Wren J. Cobb, L/Wren L. Taylor, L/Wren H. Walton; front row: Wren S. Whittle, 2/O C. Watterson, L/Wren T. Roberts.

The Royal Marines Bands

The fact that Eastney was the home of the Portsmouth Royal Marines Band added a special character and quality to barracks life. The Band provided the music and spectacle for ceremonial and social events. And it was not just the men in the Barracks who benefited from their presence: the residents of Eastney village also relished the weekly Church Parade. When the Band left St Andrew's Church and returned to the Barracks via Henderson, Bransbury and Eastney Roads, crowds lined the roads, people watched from upstairs windows of their houses and little boys marched alongside the Bandsmen. Of all the memories of the Barracks recalled by local residents, the Band's return from Church Parade remains the fondest and most vivid.

The first band at Eastney was the Royal Marine Artillery Divisional Band, formed in 1861. In 1865, now in the newly built Barracks, the Band had 46 musicians and eight boy musicians. They had a distinctive navy-blue uniform with horizontal gold-braided bars on the tunic and a broad red stripe down the trousers. Their counterparts, the Portsmouth Divisional RMLI Band at Forton Barracks, Gosport, wore a scarlet tunic with a thin red stripe on the trousers. The RMA Divisional Band played at all ceremonial occasions at Eastney but they also performed outside the Barracks, giving concerts in Portsmouth and on Clarence Pier. For the funeral of Queen Victoria, the Band was on duty at Clarence Yard, Gosport, when the coffin and royal party arrived from Cowes. In 1910 the Band went into the recording studios to produce four discs for the Pathé Company.

In 1904 King Edward VII made the RMA Band the permanent Royal Yacht Band. The Band had served on the Royal Yacht in 1902 on a cruise in the English Channel and in the following year on a cruise to

The RMA Band leads a ships' Detachment draft to the dockyard, 1905.

Ireland. However, the choice of the RMA as the permanent Royal Yacht Band was a blow to the Portsmouth Division RMLI Band led by Lt. George Miller. The RMLI Band had been a great favourite of Queen Victoria's and they had also served on cruises in the Royal Yacht. Whatever the reason for the slight, the RMA Band now had to send 20 musicians off on Royal Yacht duty for about four months a year.

Although service in the Royal Yacht was a great honour, there was a potential disadvantage. Musicians regularly supplemented their small service wages by playing at private engagements around Portsmouth, and being away for long periods could be detrimental to their personal finances. Therefore the King agreed that an additional shilling a day should be paid to the musicians serving on the Royal Yacht.

Eastney was fortunate in having some outstanding Bandmasters and Directors of Music, particularly B.S. Green and Vivian Dunn. Bandmaster Benjamin S. Green joined the RMA from the 10th Hussars in 1897. During his following 22 years' service at Eastney, Green raised the standard of music with the RMA Band, leading the Royal Yacht Band on many successful occasions.

While the RMA Band was going from strength to strength under Bandmaster Green, another, quite separate, organization appeared at Eastney. The Royal Marine Band Service was created in 1903 with the sole purpose of providing musical support for the Royal Navy. Previous naval bands serving on HM ships had proved to be unsatisfactory. Henceforward the naval bands would be replaced by Royal Marines bandsmen.

With the new Band Service was created the Royal Naval School of Music (RNSM), which was intended to be based at Chatham. The School of Music was temporarily housed at Eastney Barracks in 1903 but as the move to Chatham never came about, it remained a feature of Eastney until 1930.

In July 1904 the first trained musicians left Eastney for embarkation in several ships' bands. The School of Music rapidly outgrew its accommodation in the former Married Quarters. By the end of 1904, 700 Musicians and Band Boys had entered the RNSM. This led to a system whereby they undertook their early training at divisional bands, then came to Eastney to complete their training before embarkation.

In 1909, the accommodation having been increased, the whole School of Music was at Eastney, with a Band Service totalling 1300 serving in 52 bands afloat. The School of Music now occupied most of the northern part of the Barracks (now Lidiard Gardens) and had its own parade ground (later partly built over with a cookhouse and dining halls). Lidiard Gardens was named after Major H.E. Lidiard, known as 'the father of the Royal Marine Band Service' due to his long service and influence on the formative years of the RNSM (1903 1919).

Daily life for a Musician or Band Boy was fairly tough. George Moody joined as a Band Boy in 1921. He recalls his first days:

I was billeted in Room 45, the recruits' room, and what a reception I received. Dressed in my orphanage uniform, chocolate colour, white collar with black bow and a blue glengarry cap, I was nicknamed 'The Chocolate Soldier'. What a horde of toughs my fellow Band Boys were. They gave me lots to think about, and how to cope with all the rough handling, etc., but being well equipped with discipline I managed to steer clear of trouble.

I soon got into the routine and began to find life more pleasant, and I was in my element in the gymnasium and on the playing field. It was almost a month before I was fitted with a uniform, during which time I attended school each afternoon. I passed my third and second school certificates and also passed out of the gym and swimming. To pass out of swimming one had to swim seven lengths of the bath in a duck suit. All this month was devoted to infantry drill – standing to attention, left and right turn, saluting on the march, etc.

Musician W. Power adds to the picture of daily life:

Memories of our meagre rationing days before the 1914–18 war: ... bread and meat, plus tea and cocoa.... We could buy margarine from outside shops, real beef dripping from the cookhouse, and a bright spot during the winter months only, to buy from the cookhouse during the fifteen minutes' standeasy break from 11 am until 11.15 am, a basin of good substantial Navy pea soup. If we wanted jam we had to buy it.

Other items which had to be paid for were deficiencies in kit, also items of uniform not kept up to respectability for ceremonial parades, and to rub it in, and not in the issue, was a walking-out cane and white cotton

The Royal Marine Artillery Band, 1884

The RMA, led by the Band, marching to church in 1902

RMA drum major, c. 1896

gloves. A Band Boy couldn't possibly get past the sergeant on the gate without these last two items, and the gloves had to be spotlessly clean. All had to be found, some voluntary, some compulsory, out of one's pocket money of 4s. 8d. per week; if on stoppages, 1s. 9d. per week.

Bed-filling, for the new recruit, was a very hard task for one so young and small, but became a huge skylark as one became older and stronger, besides this was time off from musical instruction or practice. The bed-filling did not altogether finish up with a clean palliasse with fresh straw, for on the following morning it needed to be folded in half and strapped together with a 6- or 7-foot leather strap; the folding was itself very difficult indeed, and was obtained by the use and persuasion of a long broomhandle, and was finally passed as satisfactory by the duty officer inspecting the room the following morning. If not up to standard, it meant a refilling in one's own time.

During the 1920s, Eastney still had two separate musical branches on one site: the Royal Marine Band Service, providing bands for Sea Service, and the Divisional Band, supplying the needs of the Royal Marines in Portsmouth. (In 1924 the RMA Divisional Band became the Band of His Majesty's Royal Marines, Portsmouth Division.) The two branches rarely worked together. The School of Music conducted its own parades, which meant that Eastney had two Church Parades on Sundays. The Portsmouth Division Band formed up on the main Parade Ground and marched the Marines to St Andrew's Church via the front of the Officers' Mess. The RNSM formed up on its own Parade Ground headed by its own band and marched to the church via the main gate and Henderson Road. Both bands arrived at the church at the same time.

In 1930 the Royal Naval School of Music moved to Deal, Kent. About 250 officers and men, led by the Portsmouth Division Band, marched out of Eastney Barracks to Fratton Station to a train for Deal.

The RMA Divisional Band, with Captain B.S. Green, pose with their orchestral instruments in the Edwardian era.

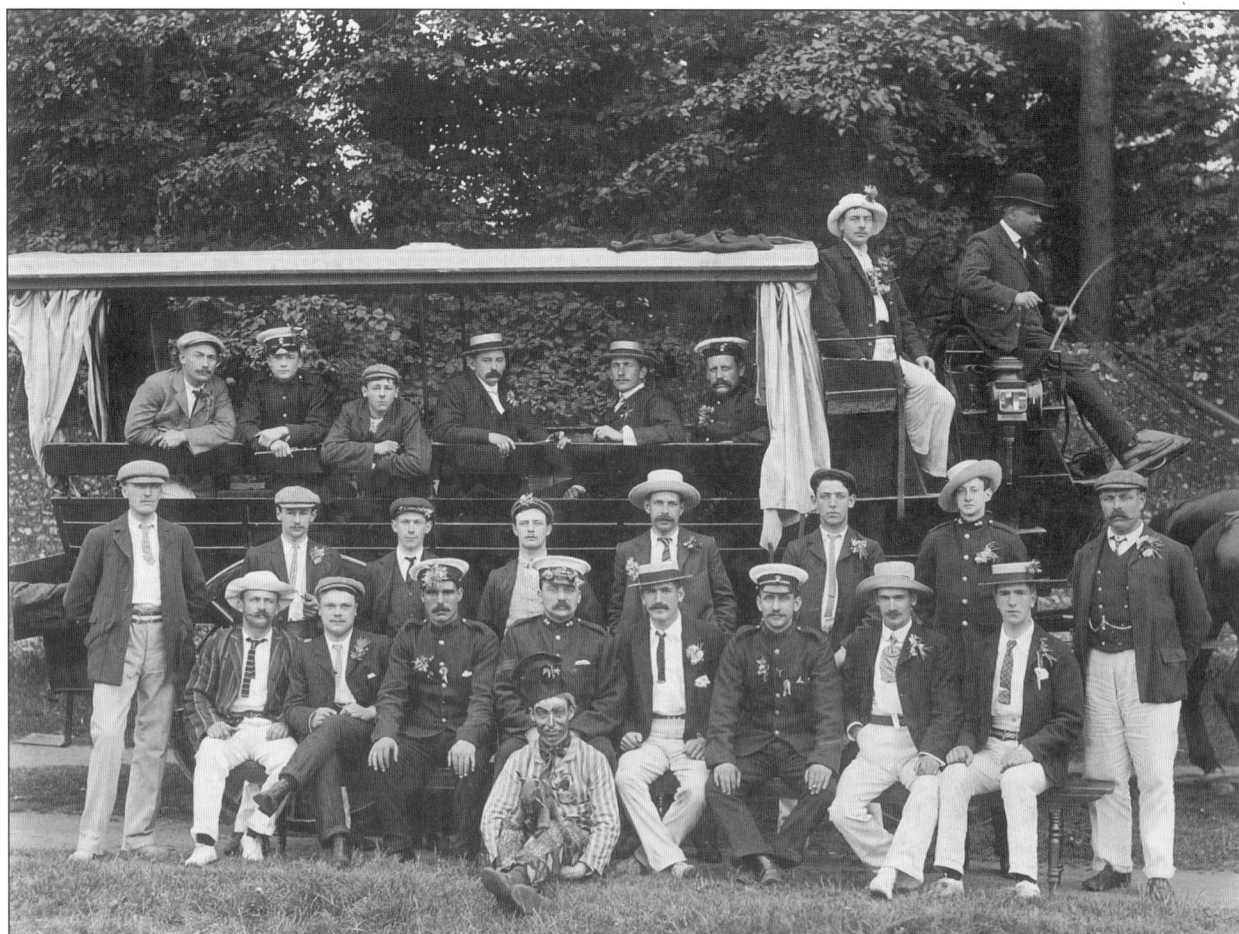

The RMA Band annual outing, July 1906

In September 1931 Lt. Francis Vivian Dunn was appointed Director of Music for the Portsmouth Band. He was only 22 years old. Vivian Dunn, the most famous figure in the history of the Royal Marine Band Service, had an illustrious career lasting 37 years, of which 22 were spent at Eastney. He was the master of the big event. In 1935, at the King's Birthday Parade on Southsea Common he conducted the massed bands of the RM Divisional Band, three Royal Naval School of Music bands and three army bands. In 1938 there was a massed bands' Beating Retreat on the Portsmouth Guildhall's Square, a foretaste of the famous Beating Retreat in Horseguards Parade, London. Sir Vivian (he was knighted in 1968) was also a talented musician and composer with many well-known marches to his credit. He left Eastney in 1953 to become the Principal Director of Music and to lead the new, unified Royal Marines Band Service at Deal.

From the end of the Second World War until the closure of Eastney in 1991, the Portsmouth Band continued its busy schedule of duties. Queen Elizabeth's extensive tours of the Commonwealth meant a considerable commitment to duties on board *Britannia*. There were many prestigious local and national events as well: the Freedom of Portsmouth ceremony for the Royal Marines held in 1959, the Corps Tercentenary in 1964, the 1966 World Cup Final at Wembley and Remembrance events at the Albert Hall and the Cenotaph, to name but a few.

In the final years of Eastney Barracks, when there were only 200 Royal Marines in total on the site, the Band remained there, alongside the Headquarters Training, Reserves and Special Forces. Their accommodation was the former WRNS block and rehearsals were held in the disused St Andrew's Church. On 31 October 1991, the Band led the final march out of Eastney.

RMA Bugler, c. 1918

Captain B.S. Green and his wife. Captain Green led the RMA Divisional Band for 22 years.

RMA Buglers relaxing after a swim, 1921

The concert orchestra of HM Royal Marines (Portsmouth Division), c. 1925

The Royal Naval School of Music tutors, with the Divisional School building in the background, 1907

Boy Buglers of the School
of Music in 1919

Boys of the School of Music on mattress-filling duty, 1911

A band of the School of Music, c. 1920

Returning to the School of Music from Church Parade, Cromwell Road, 1919

Lt. Vivian Dunn had a long and distinguished career with the Royal Marines Band Service. For his outstanding contributions as an innovator and organizer and as a musician and composer, he was knighted in 1968, the first military musician to be so honoured.

Sir Vivian conducting the Royal Marines Portsmouth Group Band during a rehearsal in 1968

HM Royal Marines CINCNAVHOME (Commander in Chief, Naval Home) Band lead the final departure of the Royal Marines from Eastney, 31 October 1991.

The Cadet Corps

For 90 years Eastney Barracks was the home of the Portsmouth Royal Marines Volunteer Cadet Corps. The Corps was founded on 14 February 1901, for the benefit of the sons of Royal Marines (in the 1920s it included civilian children). The *Hampshire Telegraph* glowingly reported that it was formed 'with a view to instructing the young generation in drill, discipline, rifle shooting and gymnastics, which all authorities are agreed as being about the most important for ensuring the vigour of the nation'.

Taking the motto 'Manners Maketh Man', the Corps rapidly grew to 150 members by 1902. The uniform was khaki with bandoliers, belts and leggings. The boys, aged between ten and fifteen, met for two hours a week, in the RMA Gymnasium in winter and on the Drill Field in summer. The annual summer camp, held in places like the New Forest, lasted a week.

The flourishing Cadet Corps attracted respect and pride within Eastney. Cadets were present at the coronation of Edward VII in August 1902, they marched past the King on his visit to Eastney in February 1904 and they were inspected by the Prince of Wales in March 1904.

The Cadet Corps remained in its original form until 1930, when it was re-formed as the Roymar Boys' Club. The club was disbanded in 1939 for the duration of the Second World War and re-formed in April 1945. Two years later the members received their first Colours. The new RM Volunteer Cadet Corps undertook more practical training in small arms, seamanship, First Aid, signals, PT, drill, map-reading and sport. Once again the Corps flourished; it had a new drum and fife band in 1952, which played at such prestigious events as the Royal Tournament and Wembley Stadium, and its first Tattoo at Eastney in 1957.

When Eastney Barracks closed in 1991 the Cadet Corps moved to HMS *Nelson*, where it continues to thrive.

Cadet Sergeant McEwen in 1901. The slouch hat was a distinctive feature of the first Cadets' uniform.

The Cadets' 7-pounder guns were used for drill displays.

Cadets perform 'The Last Stand' in Eastney theatre, 1907.

Members of the Girls' Ambulance Corps and the Cadet Corps dressed for a pageant in 1905

The Girl Cadets, Portsmouth Company, 1929

*Both Corporal Draper and her brother were
in the Cadet Corps, c. 1932.*

The Cadet Band at the opening of the Royal Marines Museum in 1975

Cadets put on a field-gun display for the 1986 Eastney Tattoo.

VIP Visitors

The Prince and Princess of Wales leaving the Officers' Mess on 16 March 1904 to lay the foundation stone of St Andrew's Church

Inspection of the RMA Division by HRH The Prince of Wales (later George V)

Winston Churchill, as First Sea Lord, inspects the RMA in 1912.

HRH Prince George at the Presentation of New Colours, 1931

A rare photograph of Edward VIII during his brief reign, visiting Eastney in 1936

George VI presents the King's Badge to Marine F. Woods of 353 Squad, 19 December 1939 at Eastney. This is the only occasion on which a monarch has personally presented the award.

HRH The Duke of Edinburgh as Commandant General at the Presentation of New Colours, Eastney, 23 April 1956

Lord Mountbatten is welcomed to the Royal Marines as a Colonel Commandant, 27 October 1965.

Lord Mountbatten at the Royal Marines Association Reunion at Eastney, September 1966

Sport

The Royal Marine Artillery Shooters had an outstanding year in 1899, winning the Excellent's Challenge Cup, Southern District League Cup, Diamond Jubilee Trophy, Duke of Coburg's Challenge Cup, Army and Navy Cup, Officers' Past and Present Cup and the RM 'All Comers' Challenge Cup.

RMA champions, 1900. Corporal G. Waterman (right) was the five-mile cycling champion.

*Runners from the Royal Naval
School of Music Sports Team, 1913*

*The RMA Bayonet Combat Team in 1913 after winning First Prize at the Royal Naval and Military Tournament
in London*

The RMA Boxing Team 1918, made up of Buglers from the RMA Band

NCOs' cricket team versus their wives, Eastney, July 1917

RMA Cricket XI, 1911

Bowls on the officers' lawn, c. 1918

The RMA teams for the 12-pounder Guns Crew competition, Portsmouth Garrison sports, June 1900

RMA Band and Buglers Company Athletics Champions, 1918

Above and opposite: the Portsmouth Royal Marines Field Gun Crew put on a display at Eastney before the Royal Tournament, c. 1927.

The 1948 Royal Marine Officers Howitzer Crew, winners of the Brickwood Trophy and Sub-Lieutenants Cup, Whale Island Tournament. Left to right, back row: Lieuts J. Beadle MC, J. Clarke, E. Potts, J. Stewart, C/Sgt Houghton, Lieuts R. Bavin, P. Griffiths, M. Baizley, D. Barton; front row: J. Maitland-Ward, A. Eyre, M. Roche-Kelly, J. Fothergill.

The Royal Marines Field Gun Crew, Whale Island Tournament, 1950, winners of the Brickwood Trophy, Sub-Lieutenants Cup and Ratings Bowl

1948–9 Portsmouth Group Royal Marines football team.

Participants at a fencing proficiency course at Eastney, 1976. Left to right, back row: Mne I. Bilsand, A.B. Probyn, POPT B. O'Fuwell, Mne P. Clifton, Sgt J. McDonought; front row: Wren P. Young, Wren C. Frey, WO1 W. Neilson, PPO B. Phipps, L/Wren Smithson.

Gunnery Training

The Royal Marine Artillery, the Eastney Marines, were raised in 1804 to man the mortars on bomb-vessels. So began a long association between the Royal Marines and naval gunnery that reached a high point at the Battle of Jutland (1916) and again in the triumphs of the Second World War. The first gun drill battery at Eastney was built in 1859. Known as the Garden Battery, it was situated near the present caravan site and its 64-pounder guns fired at targets in Langstone Harbour. In addition there was a battery of two 10-inch and one 13-inch mortars. These were the types used in the Crimean War. The original mortars from the battery are now in the grounds of the Royal Marines Museum.

Near the Hayling Ferry was another Sea Service battery, which is thought to have comprised 32-pounder Smooth-Bore guns. It ceased to function after 1876, by which time the main Sea Service Battery had been built. This was a major development, containing one 10-inch, one 9-inch, one 8-inch and some 7-inch Rifled Muzzle-Loading (RML) 64-pounder guns, all on the broadside. In addition there were two Rifled Barrel-Loading (RBL) 40-pounders, one or two 20-pounder Armstrongs and some Nordenfelt machine-guns. The big guns, the 64-pounders, were fired from the battery at moored targets out at sea.

In 1885 the broadside guns were supplemented by a more powerful 6-inch Breech-Loading (BL) 80-pounder Armstrong, and in 1896 a machine-gun battery was added, alongside the main battery; this featured a 3-pounder Hotchkiss. Apparently the noise from the corrugated iron roof and sides was terrific.

By 1898 the Muzzle-Loading guns had been replaced in the main battery by two 6-inch Quick-Firing (QF) guns in casements and one 4.7-inch QF. However, such was the pace of gun technology that in 1913 the mighty 12-inch gun turret was introduced. The focus of gunnery training for thousands of Royal Marines, the 12-inch turret became known as 'the home of the screaming shells'.

In 1947 gunnery and naval training for the Corps was centralized in the Gunnery School, Eastney. Naval training consisted of seamanship, damage control, ship fire-fighting and naval gunnery. The school functioned as a unit, with its own Commandant, Staff Officers and 40 gunnery instructors, and was divided into two sections: a long-range section and another for close-range instruction, which included anti-aircraft guns.

A long-overdue modernization of the Sea Service Battery came in 1949. The old 6-inch Mark 12 guns were removed after 30 years' service. In their place came two triple 6-inch Mark 23 mock-up turrets. Nearby the Battle Teacher (a simulator for gunnery training) was fitted with modern sound effects, which were extremely loud. In 1949 two thousand all ranks were passing through training at the Gunnery School. The improvements to the training aids continued in 1951 with a rolling platform carrying two power-operated turrets with gyro gunsights, better films, bigger and better sound effects and an electronic hit recorder.

However, the investment was short lived. By 1956 there were only some twenty Detachments in major warships and a dozen in smaller ships, totalling two thousand Royal Marines in all. On 30 June 1958 the Gunnery School closed down and gunnery training transferred to HMS *Excellent*.

Six-inch gun drill at the Sea Service Battery, c. 1903

The lecture room in the Sea Service Battery in the 1890s

Officers on the gunnery training course at Eastney, c. 1900

Machine-gun practice at the gun battery, 1890s

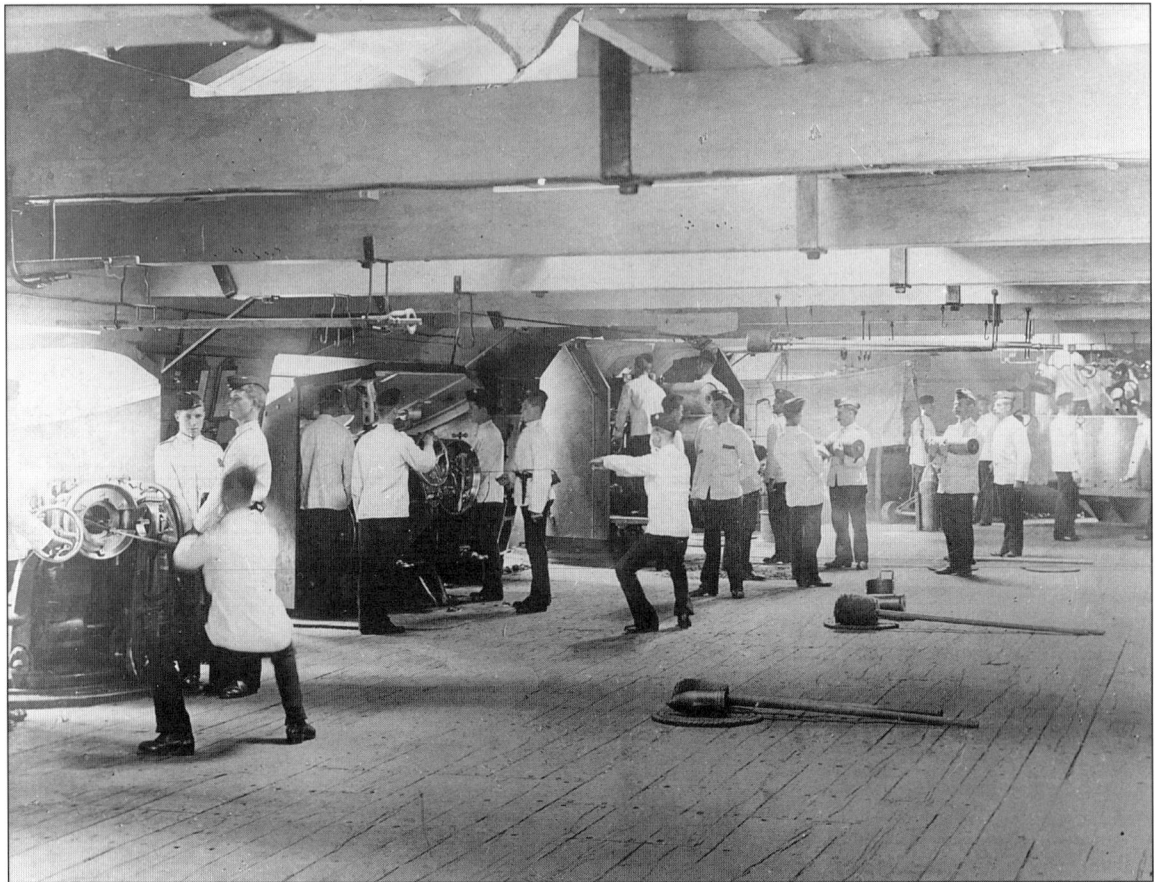

Gunnery practice in the Sea Service Battery, c. 1910

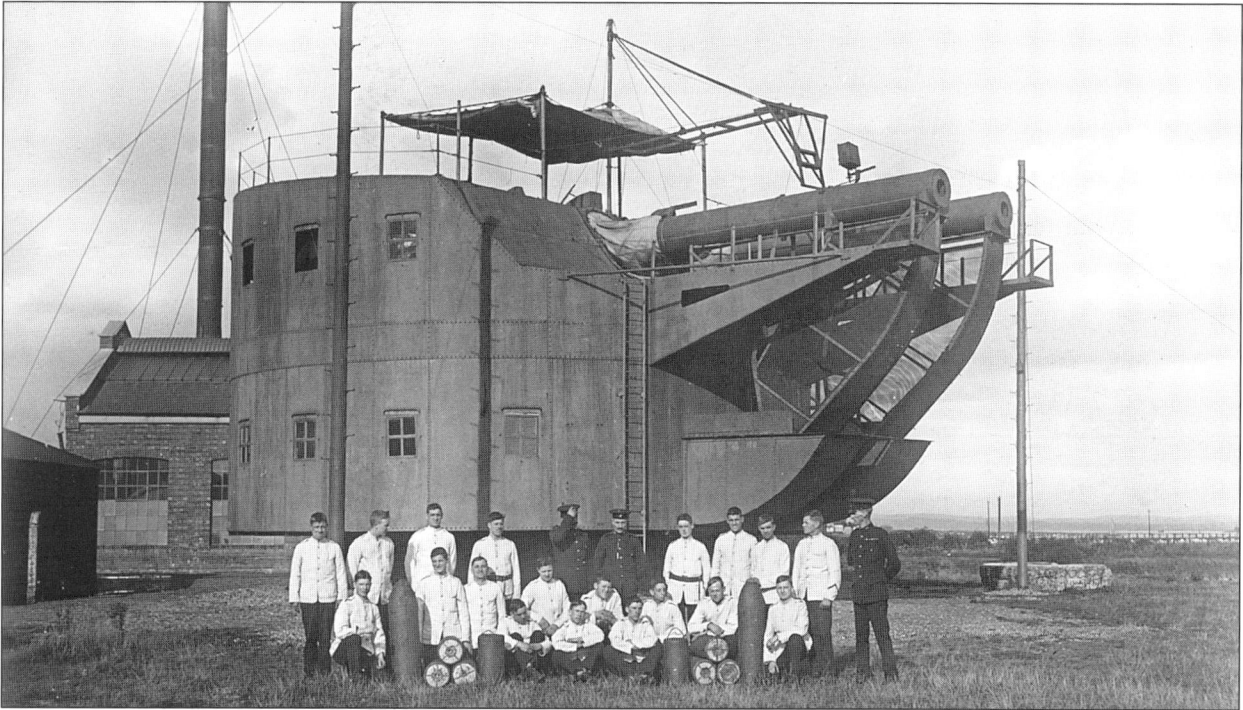

The huge gun drill turret at Eastney Barracks. Twelve-inch guns were installed in 1913.

Drill at the anti-torpedo boat guns

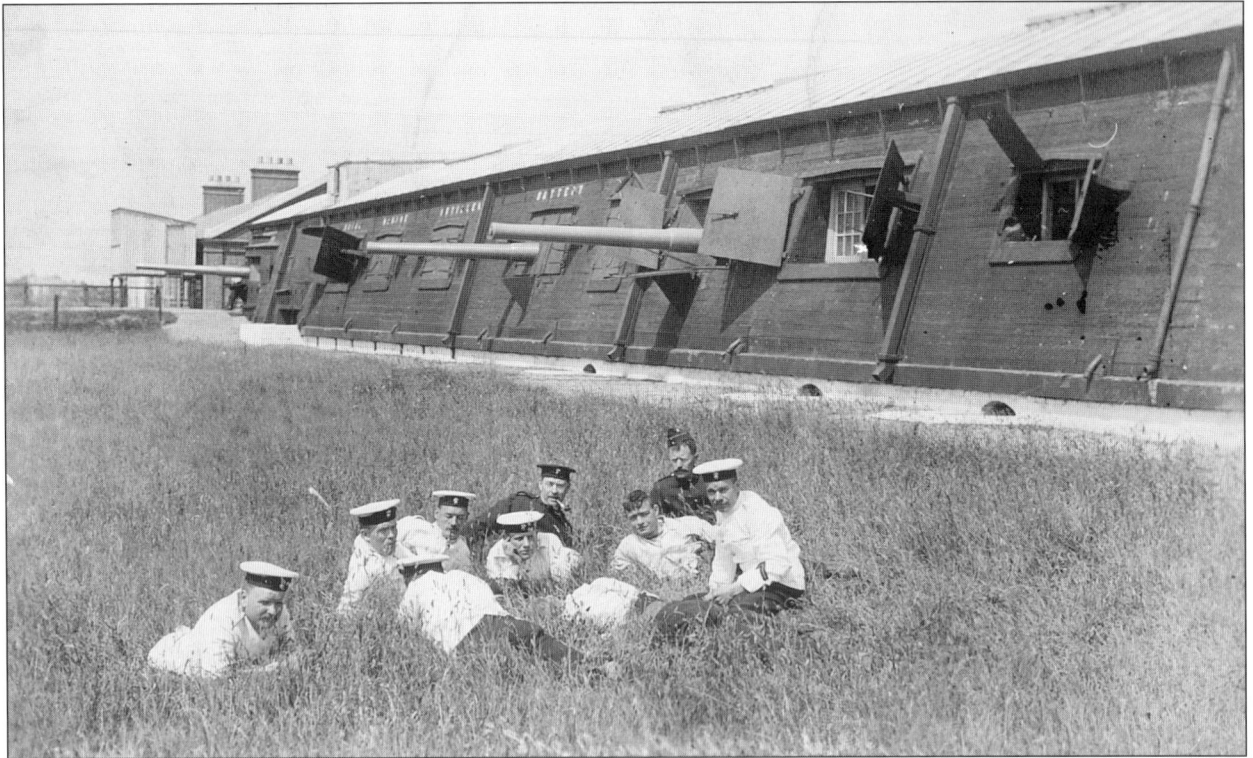

The Sea Service Battery, 1914

Instruction in shells and explosives at the Gunnery School, c. 1950

Fort Cumberland

Fort Cumberland, situated at the entrance to Langstone Harbour, was named after the Duke of Cumberland, of Culloden fame, the third son of George II. The original fort was built in 1746 but by 1785 the work began to create a large, formidable star-shaped fortress. Nearly 700 convicts were brought in as labour and their prison hulks were moored in Langstone Harbour. The main construction work was completed by 1803, although additional work was going on seven years later when there was an unsuccessful attempt by convicts to make a mass escape. The Fort was built of bricks made from Langstone Harbour clay and kilns were built near by.

As a fort, Cumberland was considered useless. The historian Edward Gibbon wrote the following epigram after visiting it: 'To raise this bulwark at enormous price, The head of folly used the hand of vice' ('vice' being a reference to the convict labourers).

The first Royal Marine association with the Fort came in June 1817, when four companies of the RMA were temporarily stationed there. In 1824, when the RMA was formally transferred from Chatham to Portsmouth, a small Detachment went to the Fort. During the 1830s the Marines practised there with mortars and Congrieve rockets. Having left the Fort in the 1840s, the RMA returned when it became their Headquarters in 1859. The Fort had belonged to the War Department, but a year earlier it had been exchanged for the Admiralty's Gunwharf site. Fort Cumberland remained RMA Headquarters until the completion of Eastney Barracks, when it moved out but kept the Fort for gunnery instruction.

Life in the Fort was basic and the damp casements made it a rather dreary existence. However, the Victorian Royal Marines made the best of it by building a skittle alley and a theatre. The officers had five-ball courts and enjoyed boating. A nine-hole golf course was built around the Fort in 1892.

Fort Cumberland in 1971. The Frazier Battery radar research establishment can be seen top left.

The Fort was also where artillery drill, known as Repository drill, was taught: training in the skills required to disassemble artillery pieces and move them ashore by cranes and joists or by creating piers and bridges.

During the First World War a 15-inch howitzer was installed at the Fort for training purposes. To transport each of these massive guns required five 100-horsepower tractors. These Foster-Daimler tractors were used at the Fort for training drivers. A Royal Marine Howitzer Brigade would later see action in the Western Front.

In 1923–4 the Mobile Naval Base Defence Organisation (MNBDO) experimental unit was established at the Fort. The idea behind the MNBDO was the creation of advance bases – in any part of the world – which could quickly be secured for defence. The experimental unit was to develop techniques for landing heavy guns to defend these bases. By 1940 the MNBDO was a firmly established unit and during the war four thousand men were trained at Fort Cumberland for this work.

While Eastney Barracks escaped damage during the Second World War, Fort Cumberland suffered tragic losses in an air attack on 26 August 1940. The Luftwaffe dropped 78 bombs on the Fort, which was accommodating about three hundred men at the time. Eight men were killed when the North East Casement was struck.

Marines hoisting a gun barrel with an 18-foot light gyn in the early 1900s at Fort Cumberland

The end of an exercise to construct a trestle bridge, Fort Cumberland, c. 1910

Royal Marines at Fort Cumberland lifting a 10-inch ML gun with 60-foot sheers, c. 1910

Building a swimming raft at the entrance to Langstone Harbour, 1899

Parade at the School of Land Artillery, Fort Cumberland, 1921

A 100-horsepower Foster-Daimler tractor at Fort Cumberland in 1915

Trials of the utility tractor by the MNBDO, 1934, with Hayling Island in the background

Another of the 1934 tractor trials at Fort Cumberland, this time towing a field cooker

Damage sustained at Fort Cumberland during bomb attacks by the Luftwaffe in August 1940

A mounted machine gun for towing by motorcycle, Fort Cumberland, 1942

The Amphibious School

After the war, Fort Cumberland became the home of the Amphibious School. This organization began to absorb the many disparate wartime raiding and amphibious units to become a strong central focus. In 1949 it took in the Combined Operations Beach and Boat Section (COBBS) which had already absorbed wartime units specializing in frogmen, canoe raids, airborne operations, attacks on bridges and reconnaissance behind enemy lines. The COBBS unit at the Amphibious School was called the Small Raid Wing. The Wing continued to develop its clandestine work and by 1951 it had been renamed the Special Boat Wing. Swimmer-canoeists were trained in techniques of small-scale reconnaissance and offensive raids. Activities included the handling of dories, various types of canoes, surf boats and paddle boards. The first parachute descent into water took place in the Solent in April 1951, adding parachuting to the training. No. 1 Special Boat Section (1SBS) was stationed at the Amphibious School. In those days of low security, the SBS frogmen could still be in great demand for demonstrations at 'Navy Days', fêtes and regattas around the country.

Alongside the Special Boat Wing, the Amphibious School had the Landing Craft Wing and Beach Wing. Crews were trained for the three main types of minor landing craft: the LCA (assault), LCM (mechanized) and LCP (personnel). Other types of training craft were crash boats, dories and pontoons. To maintain the craft and other equipment there was a large group of Royal Navy ratings and officers.

The Beach Wing had three cadres: the Royal Naval Beach Control Party (RNBCP), Landing Craft Obstacle Clearance Unit (LCOCU) and the Landing Craft Recovery Unit (LCRU). All these units had a wealth of experience behind them from the D-Day landings and they continued to develop their clearance techniques with new methods and equipment.

The Amphibious School put on many demonstrations around Fort Cumberland, Langstone Harbour and the Solent. They also went on exercises in Dorset and Scotland.

In 1951 a major spectacle called 'Exercise Runaground' on the Solent and Eastney beach was intoduced. The aim was to demonstrate a possible sequence of events in an amphibious assault on a defended coast by an infantry brigade group. The exercise involved warships, landing craft, tanks, infantry, the SBS with an arms and equipment show. Although the exercise was for the benefit of visiting naval and military personnel, members of the public could also watch the show from Southsea sea front.

In 1954 the Amphibious School moved out of Fort Cumberland to Poole.

The Technical Training Wing

During the postwar era, Fort Cumberland was also used as the base for the Royal Marines Technical Training Wing, which included instruction in driving and motorcycle riding as well as training for many technical trades. The driving branch had 30 instructors, who trained hundreds of drivers every year in 4 x 4 cross-country work, town and country driving, servicing, maintenance, waterproofing, wading, night convoy driving, accident procedure, etc.

A variety of trades were covered, including those of the armourer (small arms), bricklayer/plumber, carpenter, coach trimmer, draughtsman (mechanical and topographical), electrician (vehicle and plant), painter, printer, sheet-metal worker/welder, storeman clerk (technical) and vehicle mechanic. The value of this training facility was the self-sufficiency it gave the Corps in these areas of expertise. The Technical Wing moved to Poole in 1971 and with it came the end of the Royal Marines' association with Fort Cumberland.

Despatch riders were trained at Fort Cumberland in the postwar years. This rider, on a Triumph, was photographed at Eastney in 1956.

The Final Years

In the aftermath of the Second World War, the winds of change came to affect the Royal Marines. Reorganization and cutbacks were the order of the day. In 1950 Chatham Barracks was closed; the once unthinkable was happening. At Eastney the changes were slower.

The area between the Officers' Mess and Fort Cumberland was the first to be affected as the Admiralty took over land for Naval Married Quarters. In 1956 three estates were created. The Esplanade Gardens estate was constructed on the allotments between Eastney Fort East and the Infirmary. At the same time an estate of 50 houses for other ranks and ratings was built on the land north of the Gunnery School (Fort Cumberland Road). Three shops followed later. The third estate was built beyond the rugby pitch and Hutment Camp. This comprised the two twelve-flat blocks, four six-flat blocks and five houses called Halliday Crescent.

There were some additions to Eastney, too. After the closure of Chatham, the Royal Marines Drafting, Pay and Records Office moved to Eastney. For thirteen years they were sited in the old Gun Battery and Hutment Camp (known as Melville Camp in 1960); 43 Commando briefly stayed at Melville, then renamed Comacchio Camp, before disbanding in 1968. The Royal Marines Museum, founded in 1958, was established in the old School building north of the main gate.

By the late 1960s Britain's military and naval commitments were changing radically. Sea Service for Royal Marines was largely a thing of the past. The capital ships (battleships, cruisers and aircraft carriers) had gone from the fleet. The Royal Marines now fully embraced the commando role and Eastney was no longer needed.

In 1971 the main blow fell on Eastney. It was announced that the Technical and Signals Training Wings would leave; only the Headquarters Training Group, Corps Museum, the office of the RM journal, the 'Globe and Laurel', the Royal Marines Association central office and the Portsmouth Royal Marines Band would remain.

By 1973 the 'contraction' of Eastney had taken place. Only 200 people were left but there was a great empty estate around them. Hutment Camp was demolished in 1976 and seven years later the land was sold for private housing (the present Cockleshell Gardens). At the same time the northern barracks of the old School, Signals School and Canteen were demolished to make way for the housing estate, Lidiard Gardens.

Following the final departure of the Royal Marines from the Barracks on 31 October 1991, the site was sold to property developers; new housing was be built and key buildings converted into flats. Eastney Barracks did not disappear alogether. The new residents are still surrounded by historic sites, and Portsmouth has retained one of its greatest landmarks.

OFFICERS'
USED CLOTHING SHOP

ROYAL MARINES BARRACKS, EASTNEY

★

An Officers' Used Clothing Shop is established in the Clothing Department, Royal Marines Barracks, Eastney, controlled by the Group Supply Officer.

The aim of this shop is to provide the means whereby Officers can dispose of uniform and various articles of equipment for which they have no further use and where other Officers can purchase them.

The Officer i/c Shop will accept for sale the following articles, provided they are passed as suitable for sale by a Board consisting of a Major as President and the Supply Officer and a Captain or Subaltern as members:

Officers Pattern White Helmets	Officers Pattern Waterproof Coats
Caps	Swords and Scabbards (Infantry pattern)
Blue Tunics	Sam Browne Belts
Blue Trousers	Officers Pattern Boots
Greatcoats	Tropical Clothing (including White Mess Dress and Kamarbands, but not including khaki Shirts and Shorts)
Mess Dress	
Boat Cloaks	

All items *must* be CLEAN and FREE FROM MOTH before being sent. Provided they are so, they will be assessed for value by the Board referred to above. The decisions of this Board are final.

There is a Royal Marines Routine Order dealing with the Shop, and regulations for running it have been issued by the Major-General, Royal Marines, Portsmouth. Copies will be found on the Notice Boards in Officers' Messes.

The intention is that this Shop shall be self-supporting and, to that end, poundage at the rate of 1.- in the £ is being charged on all articles sold. To start this scheme off, the Commandant-General has lent £20 to the Shop which will be repaid when sufficient poundage is accumulated.

This shop is for all Officers' benefit and you are asked to support it. If you have any kit which you don't want or you have grown out of, send it along, provided it is in a reasonable condition. The Officer i/c Shop will try and sell it. **This means cash in your pocket and some impecunious Officer in possession of something which was of no value to you.**

Advertisement for the Barracks' Used Clothing Shop from the Royal Marines' journal, the 'Globe and Laurel', 1952

A traditional farewell to a Commanding Officer – in this case, Colonel Keith Wilkins OBE, CO of Eastney – 1983

Two views of Hutment Camp, alongside Henderson Road. Built in 1939, it was later known as Melville Camp and, when 43 Commando Royal Marines were stationed there before disbandment in 1968, as Commachio Camp.

Eastney in 1971, with the WRNS block, (lower left), the Conservatory of the Officers' Mess (centre left) and the Single Officers' Quarters in the long white hut near the sea front

A view across the northern side of the barracks to Portsmouth power station, 1958

The Young Officers' Quarters on the sea-front side of the earthbank, 1973

The Victorian former Eastney Barracks School (later the Museum) under demolition in 1983

The Royal Marines Museum was housed in the School building between 1958 and 1974.

The northern part of the Barracks was sold off in 1983 and became the residential housing estate of Lidiard Gardens ('Admirals Haven' was the developers' earlier name for the site).

The Museum was transferred to the disused Officers' Mess in 1975 and now extends throughout the block.

The Museum held a tattoo on the former Parade Ground and lawns in 1986.

The final moment in the history of Eastney as a Royal Marines Barracks. Captain K. Gill RM leads out the Royal Marines on 31 October 1991.

The Royal Marines Museum

The Royal Marines Museum, in the former Officers' Mess, seen from the Memorial Gardens

A wide range of exhibits related to the Royal Marines are displayed in the Royal Marines Museum. Behind the scenes the Curatorial Department handles the acquisition, cataloguing, research and care of the collections, and conservation work is undertaken by agencies specializing in paper, textiles, wood and weapons. Donations of artefacts are always welcomed; full details of each item received are recorded. In addition, there is an extensive stored reserve collection, which has a valuable role as a research facility. Enquiries on subjects such as medals and uniforms come from all over the world.

A number of the Museum's collections can be made available to members of the public for research purposes, by appointment. These are the Archives (including letters, documents and diaries dating back to the eighteenth century), the Historical Photographic Collection and the Reference Library, which contains Navy and Army Lists and Marine Officer Lists as well as journals and publications from 1643 to the present. The Museum also has an Education Centre, and its Education Service works with schools, colleges, youth and community groups, clubs and societies. Enquiries should be directed to: The Royal Marines Museum, Southsea, Hants PO4 9PX (Tel. 01705 819385, Fax. 01705 838420).

The Museum is open every day of the year except the three days of Christmas. Opening times are: *Whitsun to first week of September, 10 am to 5 pm. Second week of September to mid-May, 10 am to 4.30 pm*

The magnificent bronze statue of the 'Yomper' situated at the entrance to the Royal Marines Museum

Dr Gillian Winter researching in the Library

The Royal Marines Band Room display

Subscribers

Captain T.R. Abram, Royal Navy, Southsea, Hants
William H. Adams, PO/X 121159 (313), Crawley, West Sussex
Frank Agass, B.E.M., Ringwood, Hants
Mr S.E. Airey, Southsea, Hants
Major General David Alexander Elie
William (Darby) Allan, Manchester
Mr Ivan Allen, Walsall
Mr A. J. Allen, Essex
Robert J. Allen, Portsmouth, Hants
F. Allen D.S.M., Ex. R.M. CH/X 106613, Ashford, Middx
Harold Alletson, Huddersfield, West Yorkshire
Frank Allsop, Bolton, Lancs
John Ambler, Emsworth, Hants
Mne Roy S. Andrews, Folkestone, Kent
Mr R. Andrews, Cowplain, Hants
Cpl. S.L. Andrews, R.M., Toronto, Canada
S. Armour, Ipswich, Suffolk
Patricia Ashby, Havant, Hants
Brian Ashdown - Ex QMS (c), Shrewsbury
Cyril L. Asher, Dunfermline, Fife
Jim Ashlin, Warwickshire
Lt. Col. Jack Ashman, R.M.R.,Tyne and Wear
John D. Atherton, Nottingham
Mrs M. Atkins, Chingford
Mr John Avey, Poole, Dorset
Arthur E. Awcock, Canvey Island, Essex
Mr Horace Baber, Ex. Sgt. PO/X3035 Bath Easton, Somerset
Keith T. Babington, Blairgowrie, Perthshire
Colonel D.L. Bailey, O.B.E., Hamilton, New Zealand
Steve Baines, Southsea, Hants
John Paul Baker, Southsea, Hants
John W. Baker, Enfield, Middx
Major David Baldwin, M.B.E., Royal Marines, Somerset
Captain J.C. Barden, R.M., Bristol
Captain John E. Barnard, R.M.R., Cheltenham, Glos
Mr John Barnett - Sgt.(T), R.M. Ret'd, Droitwich Spa, Worcs
P.C. Barrett, Leicester
Brian Bartlett, RMA Northern Region

Mark Barton, Portsmouth, Hants
W.B. Bell, East Riding of Yorkshire
Alan F. Bensted, Welling, Kent
Harold B.Berry, FRTPi, Liskeard, Cornwall
Sqn. Ldr. E.W.J. Bevan, RAF
Michael John Billett - R.M. (996 squad), Ipswich
Edward A. Bilton, Coulsdon, Surrey
Mr G. Birch, Prestwood, Bucks
Mr and Mrs D. Birkinshaw, Barnsley, S. Yorkshire
Mne. E.J. Bishop - 334 Squad, Borehamwood, Herts
Lt. Colonel Donald F. Bittner, US Marine Corps
Frank L. Blackman, Brynmawr, Gwent
Tom and Janet Blair, Brightlingsea, Essex
John Boffin, Portsmouth, Hants
Kenneth Booth, Worcester
Colin E. Bowden, Malvern, Worcs
Mr and Mrs Charles Bowden, Porlock, Somerset
T.R. Boyne, Exmouth, Devon
Colonel G.G.W. Brace, R.M. (Retd), Saltford, Bristol
P.J. Bradfield, R.M., Portsmouth, Hants
Lieutenant (Retd) J.F. Bradford, R.C.N.R., Canada
A.L. Brend, Salisbury, Wiltshire
D. J. Brewster, Storrington, West Sussex
Richard Charles Brignall, Tonbridge, Kent
Robert C. Briscoe, Shrewsbury, Shropshire
Mr and Mrs P.D. Brook, Marine Gate, Southsea, Hants
C.K. Brookbank, Exmouth, Devon
Frazer P. Brown, Inverkeithing, Fife
Mike Brown, St. Austell, Cornwall
John (Buster) Brown, B.E.M., Tyne and Wear
Fergus J.M. Brown, W.S., Peebles, Scotland
James M. Bruce, Manchester
J. Brunel Cohen, O.B.E., London SW3
Ken (Chippy) Bryant, Malta G.C.
Mr Jim Buchanan, Tunbridge Wells, Kent
Mrs K.A. Buckingham, Tisbury, Wilts
Ex Colour Sergeant John Buckland, Ilkeston, Derbyshire
Bryan E. Buckle, Maidstone, Kent
Rick and Eileen Bucksey (Ex Sgt. R.M.), Wilson, Western Australia
Maurice W. Bugden, Burton-on-Trent, Staffs

Mr Christopher Y.W. Buist, Bury St Edmunds, Suffolk
William Bunker, Southwick, Sussex
Edward C. Bunting, Carlisle, Cumbria
Douglas J. Burford, Stourport-on-Severn, Worcs
S. Burford, Stroud, Glos
King's College Bursar, Taunton, Somerset
Carole Ann Butler (née Hoad), Sheppey
R.G. Bye, R.M., PO/X 3931
Captain Frank C.T. Baker, Gee Cross, Hyde
Mr Jack Cann, Great Baddow, Essex
Peter G. Cannon, Rainham, Gillingham, Kent
Col. and Mrs J.D.F.H. Cantrell, Trowbridge, Wilts
Samuel Carlisle, 103 Crossway, Plympton, Devon
Mr Gordon D. Carter, Titchfield Common, Hants
Jack Carter, Chesterfield, Derbyshire
Colonel B.L. Carter, O.B.E., R.M., Alverstoke, Hants
Mr Leslie Cate, Southsea, Hants
George S. Chandler, Rowlands Castle, Hants
Leonard R. Chandler - CH/X109047, Marine
Norman Chaplin, Wetherby, W. Yorkshire
Graham E. Chapman, Perth, Western Australia
Maurice J. Chave, Chippenham, Wilts
F. Cherrill, Maidenhead, Berks
Mr L.R. Chester, Tavistock, Devon
Mr Gordon Choules, Sidcup, Kent
Paul A. Clark, Poole, Dorset
Frank J. Clark, O.A.M., Sydney, Australia
Tom Clarke, 48 C.D.O., R.M., Bedhampton, Havant, Hants
Dr and Mrs M.J. Clarke-Williams, Southsea, Hants
Mr Tom Clarkson, Southfields, Northampton
Lt Col M.B. des Clayton, Sherborne, Dorset
Malcolm C.C. Clayton, Hove, East Sussex
Michael Cole, London WC2R
Captain J.M. Coleby, R.M., Crondall, Hants
B.J. (Bill) Coley, London, Ontario, Canada
D.A.H. Collin, Saltash, Cornwall
Ray Collins, Croydon, Surrey
Raymond F.T. Collins, Southsea, Hants
Commandant General Royal Marines, Portsmouth, Hants
Graham Cooke, Purbrook, Waterlooville, Hants
Major H.N. Cooper, Guildford, Surrey
Henry J. Cooper - PO/X3166, Dunkeswell, Honiton, Devon
First Officer B. Cooper, M.B.E., WRNS, Bridport, Dorset
Mrs W. Cornick, Eastney, Portsmouth, Hants
Terence William Michael Cotter, Eltham, London
Mark H. Couchman, Lenham, Kent
Mick Coughlan, Portsmouth, Hants
Robert R. Cowan, Portsmouth, Hants

Mr Stan Cox, Sutton Coldfield, West Midlands
William G.J. Cox, Stillington, York
W. Clive Cox, Langley Mill, Nottingham
Major Douglas S. Craig, R.M. (Retd), Hayling Island
Leslie Cranfield, Ilminster, Somerset
Arthur and Irene Critchley, Manchester
John Cross, London
Moira J. Cruickshanks, Edinburgh
Richard Currey, Eastney, Portsmouth, Hants
Vernon C. Davies, Waterlooville, Hants
Mr John Davies, Toronto, Canada
Ben Davies, C.B.E., Comrie, Perthshire
Mr P. Dawson, Plymouth, Devon
Arthur Dawson, Fareham, Hants
Captain J.E. Day, Eastney, Hants
Pat and Bernard Day, Leeds
Colonel J.J. Day, C.B.E., Berkhamsted, Herts
Chief Officer A.I. de Trey-White, M.V.O., WRNS, Beaminster, Dorset
Charles A. Deverill, Waterlooville, Hants
B. Dexter, Dereham, Norfolk
Ellen M. Dickson, Tamworth, Staffs
Stephen N. Disberry, Eastney, Portsmouth, Hants
Major A.J. Donald, R.M., Horndeane, Hants
Pat and Dereck Double, Isle of Wight
Captain J.P. Douglas, R.M., Canford Magna, Wimborne, Dorset
Captain P.G. Downs, R.M. Ret'd, Marshside, Southport, Lancs
Gordon W. Dudley, Southsea, Hants
Raymond B. Dunk, Chartham, Canterbury
Major P.M.H. Dunn, R.M., London SW12
Mr Frank J. Dyson, Portsmouth, Hants
George M. Edie, Bolton, Lancs
Captain Anthony Edwards V.R.D., RMR (R'd), Cranleigh, Surrey
Frank H. Elder, Downe, Kent
Leslie Ella, Cheltenham, Glos
Don C. Elliott, Portsmouth, Hants
C.N. Elliott, Skelmersdale, Lancs
Dale M. Ellis, Bedford
Julie K. Elvey, Fareham, Hants
Kevin England, Croydon, Surrey
George A. English, Ireland
Norman A. Essex, Danbury, Chelmsford, Essex
Penelope Broomer and Stephen Estrop
John P. Evans, Brundall, Norwich, Norfolk
John K. Evans, Frinton-on-Sea, Essex
Major C.J. Eyre - Royal Marines, Hayling Island, Hants
Roger M. Fahey, Huddersfield, Yorks
Joseph Fairclough, Plymouth, Devon
Cpl C.F.W. Fairey, M.B.W., R.M.B., Stonehouse, Glos

John S. Fakes, Rugby
Harry and Rita K. Ferns, Bredbury, Stockport
K.G. Fields, Southend-on-Sea, Essex
S.J. Finney, Southsea, Hants
Gordon H. Fisher, C/Sgt (Retd), Hayling Island, Hants
George F. Flanigan, Chelmsford, Essex
Jack. D. Fletcher, Lancaster
Cpl. W.R. Foord - PO/X123030, Sutton, Surrey
Peter J. Foot, Bedhampton, Havant, Hants
Jock Forrest, Prestwick, Ayrshire
F.D. Foster - (Ex 3335), Darlington, Co. Durham
(Sgt) 'Scouse' Francis, USA. malta69asprynet.com
David Francis, Portsmouth, Hants
Fred Francis, Portsmouth, Hants
Roland Freeman, Leamington Spa, Warks
Mick Fulbrook, Loughton, Essex
Mrs A.J. Gale, Southsea, Hants
Alec and Caroline Gall, Southsea, Hants
Victor J. Gardiner, Dartford, Kent
Walter V. Gardner
L. Garrett - Former Marine, Eastney 1943, Felpham, Bognor Regis, Sussex
Mr Frederick W. George, Tamworth, Staffs
Cpl. F. George - Ex PO/X3069 - 299 Squad, Lowestoft, Suffolk
M.E. Gibbard, Bitterne, Southampton
Alan H. Gibson, Malaga, Spain
David J. Giles, Hedge End, Southampton, Hants
Jack Goddard, London SW2
Mr J.A. Good, Freshwater, Isle of Wight
Captain Paul Goodlet, Chard, Somerset
Ken Graffham, New Eltham
Roland J. Graham, Carlisle, Cumbria
Dik Granger, R.V.M., Gosport, Hants
Arthur T. Gray, Dymchurch, Romney Marsh, Kent
Dr and Mrs I.J. Grayson-Smith, Gunners Row, Southsea, Hants
Robert and Betty Green, Redditch
Eric J. Green, Eltham, London
L.G. Green, O.B.E., Esher, Surrey
T.W. Grieves, B.E.M., Hartlepool
Nigel L. Griffin, Solihull
Maureen and Don Griffin, Sheffield
Charles Griffiths, Eastham, Merseyside
Mr R.W. Grigg, Nailsea, Bristol
Vice Admiral P.K. Haddacks, Teapot Row, Hants
Iain R. Haggarty, Sevenoaks, Kent
Ronald Haggis, Battersea, London
Arthur Hainsworth, Shipley, W. Yorkshire
Major R.D. Hale, R.A. Retd, Sevenoaks, Kent
Len W. Hall, Amington, Tamworth, Staffs
John C. Hall, Reading
J.R. Hall, Southsea, Hants

Captain P. Hames - Royal Navy, London W4
I. Hamilton, Beverwisk, Netherlands
Prof. John L. Hancock, Seattle, WA, USA
R.M. Hancocks, R.E., Dorrington, Shrops
Ivor and Priscilla Hardie, Seaton, Devon
Bill Harlowe, CH/X 100596, Byfleet, Surrey
J. Peter Harpham, Goole, East Yorkshire
A. Harris, Kimbeley
Michael E. Harris, Oxfordshire
R.B. Harris, Bedhampton, Havant, Hants
Ex R.M. Ralph Harrison, Doncaster, S. Yorkshire
Major General I.S. Harrison C.B., Chichester, West Sussex
Paul Harvey (Ginge), Portsmouth, Hants
Peter Hasting, Milton, Abingdon, Oxon
The Rt Revd D.G. Hawker, Heacham, Norfolk
Major A.J. Hawley, R.M., Curry Rivel, Langport, Somerset
J.H. Haycock, Martlesham Heath, Ipswich
Mr N.H. Heale, Southsea, Hants
Anthony V. Heath, Southampton, Hants
Ronald D.R. Hedicker, Taunton, Somerset
I.G. Hemshall, B.E.M., Lincoln
Mne. Hendey J. PLY-X107942, Preston, Lancs
Graham and Della Hennessy, Malaga, Spain
Mr J.A. Henshall Hattersley, Hyde, Cheshire
Colin Hepworth, Thurnscoe, Nr Rotherham, S Yorks
H. (Chick) Hetherington, Basildon, Essex
Frank Hewlett - PO/X4391, Portsmouth, Hants
Terry Hextall, Ex R.M., Southsea, Hants
Miss Daphne L. Hickson, M.B.E., London
Peter John Higgins, No 1 Teapot Row, Southsea, Hants
Major P.J. Higginson, R.M., Exeter, Devon
Edwin C. Higgs, Emsworth, Hants
Mr J.S.R. Hill, Southsea, Hants
Roy Hill, Tasmania, Australia (Launceston)
J.D. Hitchman, Abingdon, Oxon
Mr Davey Frederick Hoare-Cox, Southsea, Hants
Jane Hodge, Southsea, Hants
E.J. Hogg, Pettistree, Suffolk
Clement Holden, R.M., Croydon, Surrey
Andy Holloway, Cullompton, Devon
Freda Kathleen Holmes, Eastney, Portsmouth, Hants
Hazel and Len Holmes, Hythe, Nr Southampton, Hants
Cpl. Dave Holyoake, Portsmouth, Hants
Ron William Hooker, Barnehurst, Kent
Mr Victor T. Hooton, Bicester, Oxon
Robin Horseman, Bursledon, Southampton
S.R. Houghton, Sutton St Nicholas, Nr Hereford, Herts

THE ROYAL MARINES BARRACKS, EASTNEY

William Houston, Victoria, Australia
Mike Howard, Crawley, West Sussex
Frank Howe - C/Sgt S.B.S., Portsmouth, Hants
Jock Howells, in memoriam
Ralph Howick, Horley, Surrey
Mr Edward Howles, Birmingham
Hansen F. Howram, Eastney, Portsmouth, Hants
Peter Eric Howse, Gosport, Hants
Peter J. Hughes, M.B.A., F.C.A., Sanderstead,
    Surrey
C. Roy Humphrey, North Granby, C.T., USA
Ann and James Hunt, Marine Gate, Portsmouth,
    Hants
Major J.D.F. Hunter, Rochester, Newcastle upon
    Tyne
Tom Hurst, Whitefield, Manchester
John Hutton, London N16
Mr Maurice Hutty, Hilsea, Portsmouth, Hants
E.H. Hylands, Fetcham, Surrey
Imperial War Museum, London SE1
Ronald D. Ince, Sudbury, Suffolk
Harry N. Jackson, Dudley, West Midlands
William (Bill) Jackson, Hucknal, Notts
Mr B.G. (Peter) Jackson, Egham, Surrey
Arthur George James, Weston-Super-Mare, North
    Somerset
Mr R.F. Jarman, Letchworth, Herts
M.D. Jeffries (née Edwards), Eastney, Hants
Edith Jenkins, Southsea, Hants
Sheila and Michael Jenkins, Southsea, Hants
Dr and Mrs M.A. Jensen, Southsea, Hants
John R. Jones, Southend-on-Sea, Essex
Denis A. Jones, Buxton, Derbyshire
R.T. Jones, New Ferry, Wirral, Merseyside
Miss P. Jones, Eastney, Hants
Ron Jones, Cardiff
Sgt. B.F. Jones (BJ) ATTURM
Eric Jones, R.M., Southampton
Ronald Joyce, Thatcham, Berks
Mr Brian E. Joyles, Croydon, Surrey
Sidney George Juby - PLY/X 106293, Langton
    Green, Kent
Barry E. Julier, Yeovil, Somerset
William E.J. Katesmark, Heacham, Norfolk
Major S.O. Kenrick, R.M. Rtd, Warwick
George Kimber, Bishops Castle, Shropshire
Colonel H.F.C. Kimpton, C.B.E., Godalming,
    Surrey
Harry W. King, Plymouth, Devon
J.R. King (CPL. Rtd), Tilgate, Crawley, West
    Sussex
Richard E. Kingshott, Sidcup, Kent
Ronald Brian Kirby, Hull
Ronald J. Knight - Ex R.M. 7969, Bury St. Edmunds

Ron Knight, M.B.E., Weybridge, Surrey
Frank Knowles, Knutsford, Cheshire
Mr K.J. Lacey, Eastney, Hants
Bernard Lally, St Helens, Lancashire
Maurice Lambert, Keighley, W. Yorks
Gordon E. Lambourn, Ripley, Derbyshire
Cyril E. Lamport, Hebburn, Tyne and Wear
Ken Large, Middleton St George, Co. Durham
Mr Charles W. Lashmar J.P., Auckland, New
    Zealand
G.T. Lawrence, Canvey Island, Essex
C/Sgt R.M.B. Lawrence, Cranleigh, Surrey
William J. Lawrence, Gloucester
Lt. Col. A. L. 'Bill' Laxton, Richmond, B.C.,
    Canada
James Le Patourel Avenell, Truro, Cornwall
Edward W. Leaney, Goudhurst, Kent
Howard C. Lee, Portsmouth, Hants
David John Lee, Fair Oak, Eastleigh, Hants
Kaye and Tony Lee-Wright, Eastney, Hants
QMS (Rtd) Bill Legg, Andover
Mr Kenneth R. Legg, Swanage, Dorset
Valerie Ann Ellen Legg (née Case), Funtington
William J. Lester, Portsmouth, Hants
John Leverton, Abbots Langley, Herts
John H. Lewis, South Shields, Tyne and Wear
Eric Lewis, Portsmouth, Hants
B.S. Libby, Torpoint, Cornwall
John George Liddington, Eastbourne
Lt. Col. K.E. Light, R.M., Sydney, Australia
William John Lines, Harvington, Evesham, Worcs
Charles Little, Horsham, West Sussex
James J. Liversage, Huyton, Merseyside
Mr H. Lobjoit, Blandford Forum, Dorset
Sgt. M. Lockyer, R.M., Southampton
David Ian Lothian, Portsmouth, Hants
Mrs Mary Macafee, Bredhurst, Gillingham, Kent
Councillor J.C.S. Mackie, Lt. (M.O.), Haslemere,
    Surrey
Robert Mackintosh, Plymtree, Cullompton, Devon
Colin K. Maddox, Newton Abbot, Devon
J. Maitland-Ward, Bradway, Sheffield
Mr Ronald N. and Mrs Mary S. Mant, Southsea,
    Hants
Brian G. Marrs, Wimbledon, London
Bryan Marshall, Southsea, Hants
Reginald J. Marshall, Worthing, West Sussex
Colour Sergeant D.K. Martin, Goring-by-Sea, West
    Sussex
Malcolm P. Martin, Gosport, Hants
Major Nigel S.E. Martin, R.M., Abinger Common,
    Surrey
J.R. Mason, Portsmouth, Hants
Stan Mason (405), Exeter, Devon

Frederick W. Matthews, Barking, Essex
William F. Maundrell, Maidenhead, Berks
Peter R. Mawer, Portsmouth, Hants
Arthur H. May, Reading, Berks
George P. (Dinty) Mayes, Sutherland
J.F. Mazonowicz, Portsmouth, Hants
James McAdam, Blackrock, Co. Dublin
G.R. McCarroll, R.M. (1947–1970), London SE12
James McClymont, Bethersden, Kent
Rodney McCubbin, Annan, Dumfriesshire
Mr Finlay McCulloch, Corsham, Wilts
N.H.D. McGill, Fordingbridge, Hants
Alan McGregor, Reading, Berks
Mac McLean, Eastney, Portsmouth, Hants
Donald W. McPherson, Kings Langley, Herts
P.S. Mercier, Plymouth, Devon
Colin Mier, Littlebourne, Canterbury, Kent
C. Sgt. W.H. Millener - PO/X752, Fareham, Hants
Michael R. Milsom, Bristol
C.D. Mitchley, Southsea, Hants
Cliff Moiser, Plymouth, Devon
Ronald Molyneux, Walton, Liverpool
QMS Fred Monk, Retd, South Australia
Reginald J. Moore, Ballywalter, N. Ireland
Miss H.L. Morgan, Southsea, Hants
David E. Mosely, Oxford
Freddie Mottram, Durham
Mr Raymond G. Moughton, Portsmouth, Hants
Kenneth Alan Mumford, Great Yarmouth, Norfolk
Andrew Mackenzie Munro - PO/X120860,
  Lochbroom
H.D.B. Musto, Rustington
E.C. Musto, Alverstoke, Gosport, Hants
Peter C. Nayler, F.R.N.S., Chorley, Lancs
Mr N.H. Neale, Clocktower Drive, Southsea,
  Hants
Andrew C. Newell, Eastney, Hants
John S. Newell, Chandler's Ford, Hants
Mrs Joy Newman, Oxfordshire
Leslie R. Newport, Oxford
H. and V.M. Newton, East Grinstead, West Sussex
Mr J. Newton, Exmouth, Devon
Jeanne M. Niblett, Portsmouth, Hants
John F. Nicholls, Sidcup, Kent
Charles Nicholson, Preston, Lancs
Mike and Molly Josephine Noonan (née Case),
  Eastney, Portsmouth, Hants
Colonel P.L. Norcock, Somerton, Somerset
Luke Norcross Webb, Portsmouth, Hants
Mr and Mrs R.J. Norris, Woodley, Berks
Mr C. Nunn, No. 6 Greenwich Court, 25 King
  Street, Southsea, Hants
Lieutenant Colonel Chris Nunn, O.B.E., R.M.,
  Shape, Belgium

Captain Derek A. Oakley, M.B.E., R.M., Hayling
  Island, Hants
Mr R. Odell, East Studdal, Dover, Kent
Peter W. Osborne, Chatham, Kent
Captain K.W.E. Osborne, M.B.E., R.M. Rtd,
  Yealmpton, Devon
Prof. Denis J. Ovenden, Angus, Scotland
'Podge' Overbury, Exmouth, Devon
Robin Packshaw, London
David and Diana Palmer, Portsmouth, Hants
Mr G. Palmer, Portsmouth, Hants
Peter Parish, Midhurst, W. Sussex
Mr A.C. Parker, Westgate on Sea, Kent
T.S. Parker, Eastney, Hants
Major J.V.V. Parker, R.M., HMS Fearless
Major A.J. Parker, R.M., Lytchett Matravers, Poole,
  Dorset
Mr George H. Parkinson, Eastbourne, East Sussex
J.C. Parmenter, PO/X121162 (313), Toukley,
  N.S.W., Australia
Maurice J. Parrott, Iffley Village, Oxford
Mr Albert J. Parry, Littlehampton, West Sussex
William G. Parry, Portsmouth, Hants
Sarah Paterson, London
Mr C.W. Pauley, South Queensferry, Lothian
  Region
Warren (Whacker) Payne, B.A., West Wickham,
  Kent
Valerie A. Pearce, Portsmouth, Hants
Capt. Vic Pegler, Eastney, Hants
Charles Francis Pelligrin, Northampton
Cyril F.P. Penberthy, Keynham, Plymouth, Devon
Mark R. Penman, Fort William
Mr B.J. Percival, Alderley Edge, Cheshire
Ron Perks, Birmingham
Anthony J. Perrett, Gosport, Hants
Mr A.V. Perrior, Torrington, Devon
A.M. Philippart, Lingfield, Surrey
Frederick Philips, Henton, Oxon
Ken Phillips - RMR Portsmouth, Southampton
Jason. M. Pilalas, San Marino, California, USA
Mike Pinchen, Chislehurst, Kent
Albert E. Pitchford, Ashington, Northumberland
P. Pitman, Pewsey, Wilts
P.S.L. Pitman - Ex 41 Commando R.M.,
  Bournemouth, Dorset
Francis E. Pocock, Thatcham, Berks
Alfred B. Pomeroy, Copnor, Portsmouth, Hants
Mr W.L. Pomeroy, Bournemouth, Dorset
R.J. (Jack) Poole, Gosport, Hants
William Poole, Stone, Staffs
Mr Chris Porter, Portsmouth, Hants
Ted Postin (Ex-616 Squad), Bedworth
John A. Potter, Portsmouth, Hants

Nigel Stuart Powell, Portsmouth, Hants
Mr William Power, London NW6
Alan Pratt, Exmouth, Devon
George S. Pray, Toronto, Canada
Rodney Preston, Portsmouth, Hants
Peter Pridmore, Portsmouth, Hants
Mary Pridmore, Portsmouth, Hants
Lieutenant General Sir Steuart R. Pringle, B.T., K.C.B., London SE21
Charles Puckett, Hounslow, Middx
A.J. Pugh,Birmingham
William J. Pullen, Chipping Norton, Oxon
Mr William James Rabjohns, Plymouth, Devon
Dora E. Ray, Southsea, Hants
Frederick W. Rayers, Worcester
Mrs P.A. Rayner, Southsea, Hants
Dennis E. Read, Borehamwood, Herts
C/Sgt (SCC) A.J. Read, Rainham, Kent
Mr E. Redstone, Portsmouth, Hants
Brian A. Reece, R.M.
Stanley G. Reeves, Gosport, Hants
Edward J. Revell, Grimsby
Dick Richards, Bognor Regis
Professor Sam Scruton Richardson, A.O., C.B.E., Wylye, Wilts
Fredrick Rigby, Plymouth, Devon
Major Ernest A. Rigsby, R.M., Catherington, Waterlooville, Hants
Colin Rivington, The Colonnades, Southsea, Hants
David A. Roberts, Brecon, Powys
Philip J. Roberts, R.M., Colwyn Bay, North Wales
Mr John A. Robertson, Aberdeen
Patrick A. Robinson, Guelph, Canada
James Robinson, Eastney, Hants
Mr C.N. Robinson, Fishbourne, Chichester, West Sussex
Pam Rogers, Southsea, Hants
Peter Rogers, Havant, Hants
Don B. Rogers, Stafford, Staffs
Mr John Rogerson-McCoy, Whitehaven, Cumbria
Mrs E.M. Rose, Portsmouth, Hants
Norman H. Routledge, Wimbledon, London
Robin Rowe, Christow, Devon
John V. Rowland, Exmouth, Devon
Royal Marines Corps Secretary, H.M.S. *Excellent*, Portsmouth, Hants
James Ruffell, Leigh-on-Sea, Essex
Mrs Ailsa Rushbrooke, Essex
Mr F.W. Russell, Waterlooville, Hants
Alfred O. Russell - Ex. C.S.M., R.M., Portsmouth, Southsea, Hants
Benjamin W. Ryder, Fareham, Hants
Norman Saints, London SW20

John A. Salzmann, Aldermaston, Berks
Ms C.H. Saoul, Southsea, Hants
William J. Saunders, Copnor, Portsmouth, Hants
Tom Scade, Dunfermline, Fife
Bernard Schrier, Dagenham, Essex
James Scott, Harlow, Essex
D.J. Scott, Rainham, Essex
David T. Searle, Farnham, Surrey
Captain J.R.D. Sears, R.M., M.B.E., Berkeley, Glos
Mr and Mrs J. Seaton, Southsea, Hants
Alan Eric Selby, Farnborough, Hants
Wilfred R. Severn, Birmingham
Keith Charles Seymour, Bristol
Charles Shand, Warrington, Cheshire
P.C. Shapter, 977 Squad, Plymouth, Devon
John W. Sharpe, Sheppey, Kent
Mrs F.J. Sharpe, Southsea, Hants
Colonel Dick and Mrs Rosemary Sidwell, Sidmouth, Devon
William Simpson, Darwen, Lancs
Euan Simpson, Chester-le-Street, Co. Durham
W.J. Skates, Ascot, Berks
Captain Stan E. Skippings, M.B.E., Shirley, Solihull, West Midlands
Paul F. Slater, Burton Latimer, Northants
John Small, Spain
Mne Joseph W. Smart, Redruth, Cornwall
John E. Smee (Hull), now Bristol
Lawrence H. Smith, Copnor, Portsmouth, Hants
Bernard J. Smith, Poole, Dorset
Douglas Smith, Gunners Row, Eastney, Hants
Mr Kenneth G. Smith, Exmouth, Devon
Ronald H. Smith, Weston-Super-Mare, North Somerset
Mrs J. Smith, Verwood, Dorset
Bryan R. Smith, Salisbury, South Australia
Philip Smith, Plymouth, Devon
C.R. Smith, Southsea, Hants
Stanley Walter Smith, PO/X2068, Aberystwyth
J.B. Sneddon, Edinburgh
Maurice Snowdon, Eastney, Portsmouth, Hants
F.W.N. Soal, West Horsley, Surrey
Peter J. Softley, Eastney, Portsmouth
Margo Sonntag, Southsea, Hants
Mr Robert E.S. Spaight, RMA Tavern, Eastney
A.J. Spain, Maidstone, Kent
Geoffrey S. Spenceley, California, USA
Roy Stafford, R.M., PO/X2882, Portsmouth, Hants
Jeanette V. Stallard, Eastney, Portsmouth
Sgt (T) Graham F. Stanley, Port Talbot, West Glamorgan
Mr Harry Starling, Grimsby, N.E. Lincs
Major General P.T. Stevenson, Wotton-under-Edge
Mrs B. Stewart

J.W. Stewart, Bexhill-on-Sea, East Sussex
Captain John S. Stewart, O.B.E., FRAgS, R.M. (Retd), Olney, Bucks
Keith Stoneman, Southsea, Hants
Stuart and Angela, Gunners Row, Southsea, Hants
P.V. (Bill) Sykes, Portsmouth, Hants
Jeff and Bonnie Tall, Gunners Row, Southsea, Hants
Edward P. Tann Snr, Eastney, Portsmouth, Hants
Michael M. Tanner, Ferring, Sussex
Robert G.S. Tanner, Portsmouth, Hants
Brian N. Tarpey, Malta
Mne A. 'Harry' Tate - PO/X10007, 48 R.M. Commando, Romford, Essex
Mr K. Taylor, M.B.E., Eyemouth, Scotland
David and Geraldine Tew, Fareham, Hants
John Thacker, St Paul's Cray, Kent
Alex O. Thomas, Portsmouth, Hants
Gordon and Rosemary Thomas, Southsea, Hants
Peter. A. Thompson, Sherborne, Dorset
Sgt (D) P.E. Thompson, Exeter, Devon
James B. Thompson, Ferndown, Dorset
D.E. Thorne, Southall, Middlesex
Bryan Tidman, South Raynham, Norfolk
Bob Todd, Felixstowe, Suffolk
Howard Francis Toms, Southsea, Hants
Mr Harry Turley, Oxford
Laurence J. Turner, B.E.M., Fareham, Hants
Major P. Turner, M.B.E., R.M. Retd
J.W. Twigg (Musician, R.M.), Rugby
Eric Tyrer, Great Altcar, Formby
Cpl Bill Tyson - Ex 4501 1940, Eastney, Fort Cumberland
Colonel John A.C. Uniacke, Bristol
Brigadier and Mrs R.C. Van Der Horst, Somerset
David Vaughton, San Antonio, USA
John Venner, St Leonards-on-Sea, East Sussex
Lt Col C.J. Verdon, R.M. (Retired), Hutton, Brentwood, Essex
Mr and Mrs Peter Waight, Southsea, Hants
Alan. M. Walby, Harrow, Middx
Alan Walker, Great Houghton, Northampton
R.M. J.C. Walker - 25006 Eastney, Hants
Ron Walkerdine, Spalding, Lincs
Major General R.P.W. Wall C.B., J.P., Maldon, Essex
R.A.C. (Dick) Wallis, Lugwardine, Hereford
Stan Wallis, Cambridge, Cambs
James (Jim) Walters - PO/X116816, Bishopstone, Nr Seaford, East Sussex
Ex. Sgt Les Walters, D.S.M., R.M., Peterborough, Cambs
R.J. Walters, Former Sgt, Sandsend, Whitby
Peter M. Walton, B.E.M., Gosport, Hants

George Wardhaugh, Cirencester, Glos
Major E.H. Warren, Dorchester, Dorset
Reg Warren - CH/X4694, Kent
G.H. Warren, B.E.M, Newark, Notts
Mr and Mrs P. Waterman, Hilsea, Portsmouth, Hants
Rhoda C. Waterman, Eastney, Southsea, Hants
Mr S.J. Waterman, Hilsea, Portsmouth, Hants
Stanley C. Watkins, Southsea, Hants
Robert S. Watson, Kingswinford, West Midlands
Laird Webster, Exmouth, Devon
Jack Weeks, Torpoint, Cornwall
L. and E.D. Welch
A.W. Welch, 'former Royal Marine' CHX/113479, St Albans, Herts
Major Bruce A. Weldhen - Royal Marines, Devon, Yelverton, Devon
Ronald Wells, Southampton
R.F. West - Ex 3127, Broadstairs, Kent
Valerie Whaley, East Dean, Eastbourne, East Sussex
Major Willy Wharfe, Epsom, Surrey
Ernest Wheeldon, St Asaph, Denbighshire
Les F. White, Worcester
Eric Whitecross, Portsmouth, Hants
General Sir Peter Whiteley, G.C.B., O.B.E., D.L., Yealmpton, Devon
Mr Kenneth S. Whiterod, Bexley, Kent
Mr Roger Whiting, Norwich, Norfolk
Ray Whittaker, Deal, Kent
Corporal 'Sticks' Whitting
Allan J. Wilby, Plympton, Plymouth, Devon
Frederick A. Wilderspin, Bristol
Andrew and Rachel Wilkinson, Southsea, Hants
Christopher J. Wilkinson, Peel, Isle of Man
Major A.T. Williams, Llanrhaeadr, Denbigh
Mrs Valerie G.J. Wilson, Gosport, Hants
D.E. and G.E. Wilson, Portsmouth, Hants
Mr David H. Wilson - PO/X5454, Lewes, East Sussex
Captain J.H.G. Wilson, R.M., Portsmouth, Hants
Chris Wiltshire, Deal, Kent
John T. Wilyman, Chesham, Bucks
Gordon Winser, Byram, Yorks
Ronald V. Winslade, Ex. 48 R.M., C.A.O., Osterley, Middx
Rev. Raymond McM Winter, Norwich
Captain R.W. Winthrop, M.B.E, R.M., Radcliffe-On-Trent, Nottingham
Mr. P. Withey, London SE
John and Valerie Wood, Southsea, Hants
Raymond B. Woodham, Portsmouth, Hants
Charles Woodhouse, The Friary, Southsea, Hants
Margaret Woodhouse, The Friary, Southsea, Hants

Austin C. Woodin, Exmouth, Devon
Nick and Bianca Woodley, Southsea, Hants
Worshipful Company of Plaisterers, London EC2Y

E.A. Wright - PO/X6181, Isleworth, Middx
Peter L.E. Wye, Clacton-on-Sea, Essex
J.E. Young, Portsmouth, Hants